PRAISE FOR THE BOOK

I WILL NEVER

"I've known Jane Bateman and her family for over 25 years. When she says, 'We can have pain in our heart and a peace in our soul at the same time' I can assure you that she knows what she's talking about. *I Will Never* is the story of a mother's decision to fully embrace the unique challenges of raising and loving a very special needs son. Her story will inspire you. Challenge you. But above all, it will give you HOPE! As Jane says, "God proved Himself amazingly reliable in the precise circumstances in which I never thought I would find myself."

Andy Stanley, Pastor
North Point Community Church

"My sweet friend, Jane Bateman, has written the gripping story of her real-life experience of God giving her opportunities to trust Him in the "I Will Nevers" of her life. You will weep over her tenderness as a mother with her special needs son. You will cheer her on as she seeks to get him the help he needed. You will become angry with the insensitive bureaucrats. You will laugh with her as she has a knack to see the ridiculous in even very painful events. She is a great storyteller. At some point you may think, 'This isn't true. That much cannot happen to one family.' Every bit of it is true. You will fall in love with Jane and her sweet family. But more importantly *I Will Never* will reveal to you a mighty God who wrapped them in His love and carried them through."

Ruth Graham, Author
In Every Pew Sits a Broken Heart

"*I Will Never* will make you weep, then laugh, often over the span of a few pages. Jane Bateman's gift of sharing real-life struggles with humor and grace makes for an inspiring true story. Jane, a friend and former employee in my ministry, presents a compelling, personal account of how our Lord uses our sufferings for our good – and His glory."

Jim Reimann, author, Israel tour leader, and editor of the Updated Editions of *My Utmost for His Highest* and *Streams in the Desert*

"Years ago in Baltimore, God uncorked a tiny bottle of spiritual pizzazz and poured her over a dozen or so senior-highers. I was among the splashed. She was my Sunday school teacher, warm and soulful, tattered Bible in her lap, someone who knew about grace before grace was cool. Little did I know then that only suffering can produce her kind of artless influence. Within a few years she would step from lesser trials into mega-pain — and I thought she was deep before that fateful incident. God touched and changed me through Jane Bateman. I love her for it."

Steve Estes, Pastor, author (including *When God Weeps* and *A Step Further* with Joni Eareckson Tada

"Jane shares a heart-wrenching glimpse of God's unconditional love, joy, and tender mercies very different from the neat pretty package the world prefers. Daniel and his family did not choose his brain damage but did choose to serve God totally and triumphantly. Since my son also endured massive brain injury at a young age, *I Will Never* particularly touched me as Jane so clearly relates the bumps, bruises, and blessings of this detoured journey."

A Comforted Reader

"Jane Bateman has penned a powerful story of a journey through heart breaking and devastating experiences. It will grab you, move you, and open your eyes to how you can remain faithful to God.

This powerful story reaches out and strengthens you in the midst of shattering pain and a long journey of many disappointments. Jane, with her honest soul-searching, is the reason I am able to victoriously walk the path God has chosen for me.

This mother met Jane while on a similar journey. It is through her gripping testimony in *I Will Never* that enabled me to find the courage to hang tighter to the Savior when the circumstances are so overwhelming.

I Will Never will change lives and strengthen faith. As you read you will be given Biblical truths and promises for your journey, just as it has mine. You will find God giving you strength, courage, and more powerful faith, whatever suffering you are enduring as He encourages you in this great read. To God be the Glory, in all things!"

Sharon Patricia Reed
A mom who walked this same road, but not alone

For Larry. Many husbands and dads would have left. You never did. *I WILL NEVER* get over your dedication to our family. You are the only other person who knows how hard it was. I love you.

For David and Becky. As Daniel's siblings, you were given an excruciating gift from God. You embraced the gift rather than turn your back. You utterly amaze me. I love you both.

For Jesus. You are the only reason we survived. We give you total praise.

I WILL NEVER

For Sandy, the one who prayed
me through many a sad
Wednesday. I will be forever
grateful.

Much love,

Jane Lee Bateman

John 10:27

Jane Lee Bateman

I Will Never / Jane Lee Bateman
www.JaneBateman.com

Cover Design: Barry Burnette, Dwayne Morris
Cover Photographer: Patrick M. Clough
Cover Model: Becky Clough
Author Photo by Chad Lane / www.ChadLanePhoto.com

Scripture quotations identified KJV are from the *King James Version* of the Bible.

Scripture quotations identified NASB are from the *New American Standard Bible*, 1963, Collins World, New York and Cleveland

Scripture quotations identified LB are from the *Living Bible,* copyright 1971 by Tyndale House Publishers, Wheaton, Illinois 60187

I WILL NEVER

... chase ambulances

... leave the United States

... work with a handicapped person

... leave home

... question

... be separated

... believe God will not heal Daniel

... get used to this

... send Daniel to camp

... live through this

... go out in public again

... explain this one to Larry

... forget the Bicentennial

... lock anyone up

... get used to the principal's office

... move to Illinois

... doubt God's goodness

... lose sight that Jesus is alive and reigns

... believe God continually disappoints

... despair

... forget this Memorial Day

... forget this human sandwich

... get through this

... get angry

... accept blame

... forget this dry stuffing and plastic bulbs

... allow our home to become a battleground

... do what that church member just did

... understand saintly anonymous script

... neglect our other children

... choose between hitting and hospitalization

... stay in the ministry

... forget Champaign and McDonalds

... store my stuff

... beg for my husband's help

... allow Becky to suffer
... be your replica
... again afflict pain
... be a visual aid to my children
... play Tackle Frisbee again
... sit and stare at a therapist
... forget the ungluing
... engage in calisthenics again
... forget the candy box
... forget wounded hands
... be a loving wife
... let God remove another son
... be able to thank you
... complain again
... live this one down
... understand fairness
... shake my fist again
... cease to marvel
... believe God knows what this is like
... enjoy my home visit
... balk again
... pray again
... forget the love in the sanctuary
... play the martyr again
... soar with eagles
... finish writing this book
... NO MORE "I WILL NEVERS"
... THE END OF THE BEGINNING

ACKNOWLEDGEMENTS

A huge thank you goes to my friends who wouldn't let me quit writing, even through my moaning, groaning, stomping feet and tears — Shirley Bright, Vickie Cantrell, Katie Cullen, Debby Duncan, Jan Finley, Nancy Griffin, Pat Hickman, Jan Morgan, and Audrey Roberson. *I WILL NEVER* forget your loving prodding (and threats).

A special thank you to Dwayne Morris, Captain Outrageous. Your computer expertise wrapped in patience was just the gift God knew I needed. You never treated me like the technical doofus I am. Thank you for thinking big when I was lost in my narrow world. Your enthusiasm was outrageously contagious. I want my readers to check you out — and your book at — www.MorrisMatters.com. *I WILL NEVER* be able to express my gratitude.

Thank you, Deb Bridges, for proofing. In looking at my over-use of commas, I have decided I am quite "comma-cal." Whoops, does that period go inside or outside the quotation marks? While marking my manuscript with your little red pencil, you still found a way to cheer me on. Any mistakes you see in the finished product are of my own making. *I WILL NEVER* forget your gentle words of affirmation as I picked up the proofed copy.

Thank you to my YADA sisters for praying. Even though I am a member "in abstentia," you were so faithful to pray. I counted heavily on you. *I WILL NEVER* forget how goofy you are and yet how effective you are in praying.

To all the women throughout the years in conferences who whispered, "You must write a book." I finally listened to you.

And now for my 3 special friends who are still in the thick of the battle with children: Katie, Pat and Ann. There are no words to tell you how much I admire you. It is my honor to call you friends. I am here for you. *I WILL NEVER* stop praying for you until the victory is won.

The "*I WILL NEVER...*" Chapter 1

(or "*I WILL NEVER* chase ambulances")

The flashing lights of the rescue squad reflected against the dark in the gently falling rain in Virginia's Shenandoah Valley, much like bright red apples glistening with dew. Inside the rapidly moving vehicle were two of the people I loved most in the world - my husband and our seven-year-old son.

The Sunday did not begin with such trauma. It had been a usual busy November morning in a minister's home with three young children. "Pastor Larry" had been bustling, getting together last-minute papers (and prayers). I was threading yawning children into church clothes while mentally rehearsing my story for the youngsters at church.

The roast was in the oven, with lots of water added in the event Larry got "wound up," and the sweet-smelling rolls were out to rise. The four beds were left unmade, much to my dismay, in the interest of reaching church on time.

After church and during lunch, our second-born son, Daniel, tipped over a glass of milk that seemed to multiply into gallons as it soaked the half-eaten roast and was absorbed sponge-like into the once-golden rolls. The liquid found its lowest level into Daniel's new, brown "church shoes" and light green socks.

Daddy quietly assured Dan and his two wonder-what's-gonna-happen-now siblings, "Don't worry. There's more milk, and accidents do happen." Daniel removed the soggy footwear and laid them by the hutch to dry. His chubby, bare feet warmed quickly in the toasty kitchen where the midday sun was bouncing off the colorful, surrounding mountains.

The afternoon brought giggles as the children wrestled and snuggled on the living room floor with their Daddy. I smiled as I cleared the dishes, pondering the warm love overflowing in the other room.

That night Daniel sheepishly raised his hand during the song service at church and requested his favorite hymn. While slower would-be singers were still thumbing through the index, Dan announced the number that he had carefully memorized over the weeks. The congregation obediently sang the little boy's request, "I Shall Not Be Moved." As we sang, I silently reaffirmed to God, "Father, *I WILL NEVER* be moved nor jolted off-center. No matter what happens in my life, *I WILL NEVER* stop loving you."

During the sermon, the same wiggly little boy next to me copied the words on the communion table; "Do this in remembrance of Me." Then he added, "Mom, do you love me? I love you."

Bedtime was always a welcome retreat on Sundays for this busy mother and pastor's wife. After kisses, hugs, and extra glasses of water to our little ones, my head rested against my pillow as I reflected, "*I WILL NEVER* be moved..."

Sleep was just coming to my weary body when ten-year-old David startled us. "Daniel fell out of the bunk bed and is lying on the floor crying," he quickly reported.

I sleepily stumbled to the boys' room, assured that nothing serious could have happened. After all, there was railing on the top bunk and cushy carpeting on the floor.

Larry joined me as relentlessly we asked Daniel if he was all right. He rubbed his knee and pled, "Just let me lie down." Suddenly he fell asleep, and just as suddenly, he shrieked, "My head! My head. My eyes hurt. The light hurts my eyes. My stomach hurts...." and his voice trailed off.

Sensing the gravity of the situation, Larry called the rescue squad. I thought he was overreacting.

I hovered over this little second grader and cradled his head in my hands as he begged, "Momma, hold me." While I sought to hold him, he vehemently denounced the affection with, "Get away from me!"

Larry later described his feelings as he accompanied Daniel in the emergency vehicle:

Racing for the Interstate, my mind reeled. Alternating between praying, looking after Dan, and seeing where we were, scripture portions raced through my mind at computer speed. I reminded the Lord that I did not know what was wrong with Daniel, or what he might need, but He would have to assemble the right team to care for him. I looked up, thinking the hospital must be near, only to discover that we were approaching the exit only several miles from home.

*After what seemed like an eternity at 80 miles per hour,
we arrived at Roanoke Memorial Hospital emergency
room. Dan was placed in the Neurological Intensive Care
Unit (NICU) for observation.*

*The examination by a prominent neurosurgeon revealed
nothing. While the doctor and I studied X-rays, a phone
call from NICU explained that the dilation in Daniel's
right pupil indicated something was wrong within in the
skull. I rifled questions to the doctor as the surgery cart
sped down the hall. Dan's groin artery would be injected
with dye so more x-rays could immediately 'road map'
the problem. While signing papers giving permission for
this procedure, I was flooded with doubts. The surgeon
barked, "Just sign them. I know what I'm doing. I'm
trying to save his life!"*

I signed.

*Could this really be happening? I collapsed on my knees
in prayer and cried to my Father for strength.*

As his mother, I, however, was so convinced that nothing
could be wrong, I had re-tucked David into bed with the
assurance, "Don't worry. Dan probably won't go to school
tomorrow because he'll have a late night tonight. But he'll be
back tonight, I'm sure." Three-year-old Rebekah, her
bouncy, blond curls just reaching the neck ruffles on her
pajamas, had stood on tiptoes by her window trying to see the
fading flashing red lights before giving up and going back to
bed.

The ringing phone startled me, seeming louder at this
time of night. With a tight voice Larry stated in monotone

fashion, "Jane Lee, Dan has a blood clot. He has fifty-fifty chance of living through the surgery. Come."

I sat on the edge of the bed in numbness. I wanted my mother.

Hesitantly, I called our close friend and church secretary, Merle Mabry. I was relieved when she answered the phone as cheerily as she would have at noon, although it was midnight.

Merle and her husband, Buddy, arrived quickly at our house. Merle kept our sleeping children while Buddy drove me to the hospital. As the windshield wipers rhythmically kept time in the rain, Buddy and I made feeble attempts at conversation.

The hospital loomed large in the night, illuminated only by lights from the empty parking lot. I soberly mused, "Such a big place to find one small boy and a weary Daddy."

A security guard hurriedly admitted us into the locked lobby and, without a word from us, directed us to a lower level. I could not understand how he knew who we were.

Slowly descending the steps, my racing heart sank without warning as I found Larry kneeling by an old bench in the deafeningly quiet hall. Weeping, Larry held Daniel's pajamas and slippers in his large, trembling hands.

Incorrectly sizing up the scene, I gravely concluded that our son had died.

I was jolted as the surgery cart rattled down the hall with Dan. Intravenous bottles clanged over his head. He was not dead, but was in respiratory arrest.

Riding on the cart side rail hovering over Daniel was a nurse who was blowing vigorously into Dan's mouth. I remember being surprised at how excruciating the work seemed; it did not appear as easy as I had seen on medical television programs.

I attempted to stop the people in white as they sped down the corridor. I wanted to ask questions and get a good look at my injured son. Running in pursuit, I vainly "pulled rank" and snapped, "Hey, STOP, I'm his mother." No one seemed impressed enough to even slow down.

Undaunted, I tried to board the elevator. The closing doors seemed to mock me. Helplessly, I stood in the hall while strangers accompanied my dying seven year old.

I felt cut off. Angry. Jealous.

Someone coldly instructed us where to wait.

The archaic, small waiting room was drab and ugly. A dim light made hopes seem dim as well. It was a grim place to wait for grim news.

Clutching and shredding a tissue, her crossed leg in constant motion, a pale lady shared the dismal room with us. We became "war buddies," although we spoke only two sentences. She gave me a terse account of her husband's turning the ax head the wrong way while chopping wood and splitting his head open. She politely asked why we were waiting. I whispered, "My little boy fell out of bed." My account sounded trite after her story.

Larry had grabbed his Bible before exiting our house to go with the rescue squad. He read to himself and to me by the dull light, and as he read his face reflected comfort.

Larry later wrote to friends:

I was nearly sure Dan would die, and as God ministered to my heart, I remembered, "Permit the children to come to Me..." I never realized the scripture of my sermon that morning would be so vital to facing the offering up of my son just hours later. I was learning a little of the love of the Heavenly Father for His suffering Son. I remembered

*the Lord Jesus praying, "My soul is deeply grieved to
the point of death...and he went a little beyond...fell
on his face and prayed, saying, My Father, if it is
possible, let this cup pass from Me; yet not as I will
but as Thou wilt..." (Matthew 26:38,39 NASB)*

Waiting together, Larry and I were overwhelmed with the
peace of God, knowing that Daniel had earlier received the
Lord Jesus as his own personal Savior. We knew, on that
ground alone, our son was ready to die.

The long hours of waiting were broken only by the arrival
of our "church family." One of the new Christians
encouraged Larry, "I knew if it were my son, you'd be here
with me. I want to be with you, Pastor." The room and the
corridor soon overflowed with concerned, praying friends.

At 7 a.m. a little boy with his face as white as his gauze
turban was wheeled to us. As I kissed the unconscious form,
I felt an irrepressible urge to protect.

Before Daniel was wheeled into the Intensive Care Unit
and through other doors that did not welcome me, Larry gave
a parting shot of advice to the nurses: "He's used to sleeping
with warm pajamas and blankets."

Little did we dream he would sleep on sheets of ice for
many days.

As the long cart made the turn into the room, I silently
prayed, "Oh Father, thank you that *I WILL NEVER* go
through anything like this again."

And in my heart, He seemed to say, "Oh?"

—

7

The *"I WILL NEVER..."* Chapter 2

(Or, "*I WILL NEVER* stay in the United States")

Long before "the fall," a handsome, dignified fellow from the northern Virginia county of Arlington captured my southern Virginia heart as soon as I saw him. I first spotted Larry at a Youth for Christ Convention in Bristol, *Virginia* (says he) and/or Bristol, *Tennessee* (I say).

Three months later, as a timid college freshman, I searched in vain for a seat in the crowded cafeteria at Columbia Bible College in Columbia, South Carolina (now known as CIU). Dinner tray in hand and feeling conspicuous, I was relieved when Larry Bateman offered me his chair. I am not sure what impressed me the most, this good-looking gentleman or the opportunity to sit down. Either way, he "swept me off my feet."

A "hitch" developed in the blooming relationship before we could dream of being "hitched." I had totally committed my life to Jesus Christ and wanted to serve on the foreign mission field. My only knowledge of missions came from a magazine given to me in high school. The issue had been devoted to lepers in Korea. I purposed to go to Korea and work with these needy lepers I had read about.

When Larry informed me he was going to serve the Lord in North America, I was appalled. Had he not read the magazine? I thought, and told him, he was worldly - minded to consider such an easy field of service while I was going to the "uttermost parts of the earth." He thought I was naive and lacked vision. I thought he was carnal.

My last warning was "*I WILL NEVER* stay in the United States."

My deep compelling call was quickly re-evaluated when a missionary speaker in the college chapel service casually mentioned some inconveniences on the foreign field. Batting my eyelashes and with a singsong voice, I chirped, "Larry, God may be calling me to the States, too."

Three years later, Larry and I decided our pending marriage had a better chance of survival since we would both be in the same country.

While Larry sold shoes, Fuller brushes, and cars, I ventured to be the best little wife there was. Time will fail me to tell you about the fresh pumpkin pies I made complete with strings and seeds. (Not one cookbook mentioned first cleaning out the "goop" in the pumpkin, and I went strictly by the book) It was a bit like eating orange seaweed with sprinkles of sand in it. Larry had a difficult time thanking the Lord before our meal of Chow Mein to which I added an entire box of cornstarch. I was too tired from stirring to dispose of it.

Balancing the checkbook (or the lack thereof) was a humbling experience. My father had never filled out check stubs. He merely called the bank on Friday night, announced his name, and a teller would report his balance. I, therefore, came to the conclusion that only neurotic people filled out check stubs. My new husband, who had left a budding career in insurance to enter the ministry, was astounded at my non-bookkeeping.

The final explosion came when Larry was reviewing the month's checks and noticed I had filled in a dollar amount in the stub. The cents column, however, had question marks that I had subtracted with a resulting numerical value. Larry queried in a jutted, taut voice, "How in the world do you subtract question marks and end up with a number?"

He "cried all the way to the bank," and the vice-president tried to help him unravel the mysteries of his new bride's mind. Larry thought the bank official was tactful when he only shook his head in disbelief and did not elaborate on his true feelings.

While Larry and I both were anticipating our Bachelor of Arts degrees in Bible, Larry got his B.A. as planned. I, on the other hand, had a B.A. - breech arrival - of our eight pound David Lawrence. Larry studied for an exam between my contractions, and if he did not pass, it was not because I did not give him plenty of time to study.

Motherhood brought a new dimension of love with it that I never knew existed. My parents, my grandparents, and my husband were marvelous visual aids of love to me. But when they placed David into my arms, I finally understood a little of John 3:16; "For God so loved...that He gave..." I realized what sacrificial love meant. I understand more of what our Bible professor meant when he thundered, "God not only loves you, He just loves to love you" (I had known God loved me, but it never occurred to me that He particularly enjoyed it).

After Larry's graduation we sadly left the tall pine trees in our little trailer park in South Carolina. Following his ordination into the ministry, the three Batemans moved to the suburbs of Chicago to be trained in an open-air ministry.

The cultural shock was unnerving, and I was astounded that I had ever thought I could make it in Korea.

While I found this type of ministry difficult, Larry gloried in it. He was also very good at it. His voice boomed to the crowds as he sketched with paints or chalk. He also used simple slight of hand illusions to illustrate to the crowd the truths of the Word of God.

One glad day the training was over. We were ready to pioneer an open-air ministry in another city. I joyfully announced, "Good-bye, Illinois. Eastward, ho, the wagons. *I WILL NEVER* return to Illinois," I promised myself.

And in my heart, He seemed to say, "Oh?"

The "*I WILL NEVER...*" Chapter 3

(Or, "*I WILL NEVER* work with a handicapped person")

And pioneer we did - in Baltimore, Maryland.

Because we had no place to stay, a small church offered us the use of a three-story, hundred-year-old creaky house right next to the church. Life in this building was not without its problems. Not only did I forget the time and have diapers drying on lines strung in the church parking lot as parishioners arrived for Wednesday night prayer meeting, but in my haste to remove the laundry, I inadvertently left the door to the house open, and our dog paraded proudly down the aisle of the church during the service.

Soon after that, we did not realize daylight savings time had begun. We were sleeping on mattresses on the floor of the barren adult Sunday school room when we heard laughter and footsteps ascending the winding stairway for Sunday school. "I in my kerchief and Pa in his cap" got quickly unsettled from our "nap." We picked up ourselves, our baby, and our mattress and escaped through another door.

We were grateful for the people's loving kindness in providing us a place to stay, but we were overjoyed as we purchased our first home. And there was good news to go with the house - after May, all three bedrooms would be occupied.

Tiny, fat-cheeked Daniel James arrived on May 1st. Daniel had such chubby dimpled cheeks one could hardly resist lovingly pinching them. His eyelashes were magnificent. As he grew, his gold hair became luscious curls.

Because my involvement in the open-air ministry was so limited, I took great pleasure in teaching a group of teenagers each Sunday. Steve Estes, one of my students, had been working closely with Larry in the open air. Steve asked me if I would meet with him and a friend he was trying to disciple. His sparkling eyes and crooked smile betrayed his excitement. He explained, "If you could just teach her on Thursdays what you're teaching me on Sundays, it would be so neat. She's struggling, but she's growing."

I was delighted.

Almost as an afterthought, Steve added, "Oh, by the way, I forgot to tell you; she's paralyzed."

I froze. My mind reeled. Handicapped? I did not feel comfortable around handicapped people. Realizing that would sound ridiculous to a 16-year-old who obviously was not bothered by the situation, I shifted my feet and pushed my hands awkwardly through my hair, stalling for time.

"Oh Steve, I am so honored you asked me. But you know what would be even better? You are closer to her age than I am. And if you continue to teach her during the week, you will grow in your Christian life. And she will grow too. It will be good for both of you."

And Steve went each week.

Sure enough, Steve grew.

Joni Eareckson Tada grew, too.

Those were early days in Joni's struggle after her diving accident in the Chesapeake Bay. She had not written any books (though she wrote many later, several with Steve), nor had a movie been made of her life. Her artwork, drawn with a pen in her mouth, was not in demand then, nor was she in demand as a popular speaker. She's all that and more now.

I drove home and thought about Steve's request to me.

"I WILL NEVER work with handicapped people. I don't know how to act or what to say," I said almost audibly.

And in my heart, He seemed to say, "Oh?"

Steve Estes teaching David, left, and Daniel guitar

Daniel, left, with David showing off on vacation

The *"I WILL NEVER..."* Chapter 4

(Or, *"I WILL NEVER* leave home")

As anyone in full-time ministry will attest, it is indeed difficult to know how much time to give to ministry and how much time to give to family. Larry had worked very hard to get a balance, and David and Daniel wallowed in the attention directed their way by their daddy. Larry and David arose early to study the life of the Biblical King David. And almost-four-year-old Daniel, whom we called "Daddy's little replica," was blossoming in his own right.

The day before spring, further joy permeated the Bateman's home and hearts when we welcomed Rebekah Jane. We were ecstatic. Larry was present in the delivery room, and I realized anew how much I depended upon this dear man of God.

This was turning out to be a wonderful life.

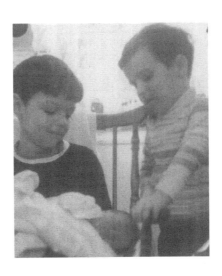

David holding newborn Rebekah as Daniel looks on

A year or so later, Larry and I, hand in hand, sat on the blue flowered sofa and watched the children playing on the living room floor. David, compliant and outgoing, directed the play. Daniel, our quiet, gentle second-born, cooperated happily with obvious respect for his big seven-year-old brother. And our sunshine-in-patent-leather shoes just went from person to person, flashing her bright eyes and smile.

The rearrangement of priorities had so dramatically affected our family we began praying for ways to share with other families.

After having served in Baltimore for six years, the five Batemans, plus Andy the dog, left for Salem, Virginia where Larry had accepted a church's call to pastor.

All our belongings were shoved, stacked, packed, and pushed into a giant, green rented truck. Larry drove the truck while I drove the car with the children. The neighborhood friends lined the streets and sadly waved their Baltimore Orioles baseball caps as we proceeded down their parade route. David and Daniel sobbed. I choked. Becky squirmed in her car seat, sensing something was happening. And although I never really asked, I have an idea there was a misty eye in the driver of the big green truck.

Hours later, nearing the Shenandoah Valley and seeing the mountains rising before us on the horizon, the reality of my new role as a pastor's wife startled me. I silently cried out to the Lord for help. God, in His loving way, comforted and encouraged my anxious heart, reminding me of a verse from a favorite hymn, "How Firm a Foundation."

> Fear not, I am with thee
> O be not dismayed
> For I am thy God and will still give thee aid;
> I'll strengthen thee, help thee,
> And cause thee to stand,
> Upheld by My righteous, omnipotent hand.

I hummed the song as our little caravan rounded the corner and wound up the hills to our brand new parsonage.

In the evening mist the sun fairly danced off the mountains surrounding our house in this magnificent valley. Our new "flock" was waiting in the front yard to greet us and to help unpack. Our name was painted on the mailbox, making official that this was our new abode.

The large, "spanking new" parsonage was breathtaking. When the sun bounced off the yellow house with the luscious carpeted mountains in the background, it reminded me how the yellow marshmallow chicks looked nestled against the green grass in an Easter basket.

Children were happily at play at a nearby park. The sounds from the park were sweet to our ears. (Those same sounds would later come to haunt us.)

Larry reveled in his new ministry as pastor. Although things were not always perfect, we felt this had to be the closest thing to heaven as these dear church people seemed so eager to learn in the "little brick church in the holler by the crick."

What an ideal life.

Love abounded from our church people as they shared their gardens with us. They kept us supplied with food they grew, picked, and often canned for us. Love abounded as well in potluck dinners with all the Southern delicacies one could imagine; love abounded during revivals and Sunday school picnics as well as hugs and kisses. The people lavished us with a Virginia ham each Christmas (is there any other kind of ham?), and I reciprocated one year by making fudge for every family in the church. By Christmas day I did not want to even smell chocolate.

"Pastor Larry" baptized many in the frosty Roanoke River. The thick, surrounding trees forbade any sunlight from warming this stream that gushed down from the mountain. It was a bright Sunday afternoon when a little fellow, who looked a lot like the preacher, met his daddy in the river to show to the world he had earlier received the Lord Jesus as his own Savior from sin. The preacher choked a bit when he said, "I baptize you, my dear son Daniel..."

My mind's eye quickly remembered the time when Dan had been so excited over his decision to trust the Lord Jesus as his Savior, he called his grandparents in North Carolina. In his toothless way, he lisped, "I just askth Jesuth into my heart." And his Grandmother Bateman wrote back this note:

My dear Daniel, I just had to write you a note and tell you how happy I am after hearing your voice on the telephone this morning. I praise God for answering

*my prayers. I went to Sunday School this morning
with joy in my heart and told my class of the good
news - that another grandson had asked Jesus to
come into his heart...Trust in the Lord with all your
heart, and He will direct your path through all the
days of your life. Jesus is yours, and Jesus is mine. So
let's stay sweet for Jesus' sake. I love you.*

Grandmother B.

It was a warm, still evening when I took refuge on our
deck. The sun seemed to hang in the sky for an extra time, as
if knowing I was enjoying its beauty and wanting to oblige
me. The sky, streaked with red, seemed to touch the top of
the mountains. I propped up my feet and leaned back with
satisfaction ringing in my heart.

I was alone, and the stillness felt warm to my soul. I
broke the silence when I softly prayed, "Father, thank you for
the sunset. Thank you that the very One who cares for
sunsets - cares for me. Thank you for bringing us here.
Father, *I WILL NEVER* leave this place. Never. "

And in my heart, He seemed to say, "Oh?"

The "*I WILL NEVER...*" Chapter 5

(Or, "*I WILL NEVER* question")

Happy summer memories of special times with grandparents were tucked deeply into each heart while new lunch boxes, new paper and pencils, and new school shoes were uppermost in everyone's thinking.

The anticipated big morning came, and David and Daniel posed for a picture. Both grinned, and David sat a little taller, realizing this was his fourth-annual-first-day-of-school picture, and Daniel's second one. Dan tightly clutched his new lunch box while David cradled a new red notebook in his arm.

I cried when the scholars left, as I always did on the first day of school, realizing the children were getting older (as was their mother). Scooping up Becky, who was still wearing cereal on her face, gave me the boost I needed to start the day.

The neighborhood was eerily quiet. Only the rumble of yellow buses that magically appeared in the valley the first of September each year could be heard.

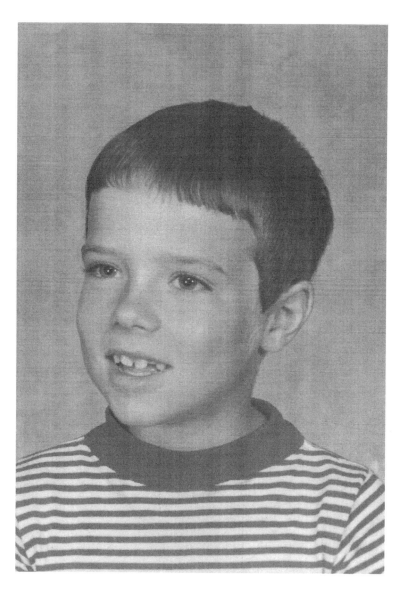

School picture not long before Daniel fell - age 7

Becky and I ventured across the street to the park. My
arms pushed her in the swing while my mind wandered to the

activity that had permeated this very park during the hot months. In my mind I could still hear the shouts from the Little League games. I could still picture David in his uniform and Daniel performing admirably as batboy.

"Momma, next summer when I'm eight, I'm gonna play, too. I can't wait. I'll be the best batter they have. I'm really good at sliding, too, Mom. Have I ever showed you how I can slide into bases?" Dan had asked daily. Even as David hung up his baseball cap and carefully placed his bat and glove in a place of honor in his crowded closet, Daniel's eyes seemed to wistfully twinkle with, "Next summer, I'll be eight. I'm gonna play."

Becky's whining brought me back to the present and we went home to fight the quiet together.

Larry was fighting a battle as well. He hobbled around on a leg cast, acquired in the ministerial "line of duty." Details are not appropriate, but he had fallen while running through the Virginia Mountains vainly pursuing someone who desperately needed help, but who did not want it. Larry had continued running several miles on his broken leg throughout the muggy afternoon.

It was a small preview of the help he would strive to give to Daniel. And this time, the miles would be many, the time spent would be lengthy, the progress seemingly non-existent, and the life-and-death situation would demand more from both of us than either of us ever realized was possible to give.

The autumn air was a bit nippy, and the mountains around us took on their gold, orange, and red colors as the whole valley appeared to be decked in a glorious headdress.

We decided to drive to another town and do some early Christmas shopping, enjoying the lingering fall leaves along the way.

As we wheeled down the aisles with mounds of toys on each side of us crying out to be bought, Dan interjected his desire in each aisle. Riding on the front of the cart, Daniel whispered, "All I want is a G.I. Joe," and David, not to be outdone, spoke a little louder; "I want everything in the store – but especially this big ranger station and a camera." Seated in the cart, Becky caught the excitement and mumbled, "Me want a baby..."

Daddy wheeled everyone on one side of the store while I stuffed a cart on the other side of the store. Then we rotated jobs.

Our station wagon fairly bulged as we drove back to Virginia. It was hard to keep little eyes from peeking under the blanket that covered all sorts of interesting boxes.

Nearing the valley, big brother David sat in the front seat helping his Daddy with directions while Becky slept in my arms (this was before car seats were a must). Dan, who had been playing with a small car for many miles, flashed his winsome eyes at me and asked, "Momma, I'm really your best little traveler, aren't I?" He was right. He was such a joy to take places and such a good rider on long trips.

I did not realize then that our "best little traveler" was to travel soon through another valley...the one Psalm 23 describes as the "valley of the shadow of death." I could not be in the back seat with him on that trip. There was only One who could stay with him.

After we returned home, David invited a friend to spend the night to celebrate his birthday. They were excited for two reasons: first, they could stay up late (I did not tell them that this was the night to set the clocks back after daylight savings time ended, and they really went to bed at the same time); secondly, they were excited because friend Jeff could sleep in the top bunk as a special "company treat." Looking back on the "company treat," I shudder.

Two weeks before Dan's fall, he and Becky celebrate David's 10th Birthday

It was only a week after David's birthday that a mission's conference was held at our church. There was a time of special emphasis on the need to reach the entire world with the Gospel. During a time of prayer with the ladies of the church, I voiced to the Lord my desire to give Him the most precious treasures I had — my children — to go anywhere for Him.

25

I had NO IDEA what God had in mind. I had NO IDEA that His "anywhere" and my "anywhere" were nothing alike. I ended my prayer, "Father, *I WILL NEVER* question You about what You allow in my children's lives. *NEVER.* "

And in my heart, He seemed to say, "Oh?"

The "*I WILL NEVER...*" Chapter 6

(Or, "*I WILL NEVER* be separated")

The mission conference over, snickers and whispers were here and there. Secret phone calls were being made. The people of our church were planning a surprise birthday party for Larry. Plans were made to blindfold him and take him via wheelbarrow "over the river and through the woods" to another building for games and refreshments. We counted the days until November 12th when "Pastor Larry" would turn 33 years old.

But Sunday, November 9th, came first. Our second - born son had fallen out of bed.

The same group of party-planners stood with us in the hall of the hospital, hanging onto the surgeon's every word. The doctor shifted from one foot to another, and I felt agitated at his mumbling. His words were barely audible, although no one dared interrupt his report with the admonition to speak up.

He seemed weary. But he cursively rehearsed the surgery. He explained he had removed a blood clot from the right side of Daniel's head. "The biggest clot I've ever seen in 30 years of neurosurgery. It was as big as a baseball. He might make it if there are no complications with his lungs or kidneys," he reported. He then urged us to leave the hospital.

Leave? I had never been forbidden to be with any of our children. "*I WILL NEVER* be separated from him now," I murmured under my breath. The sign on the door of the Intensive Care Unit screamed at me - visitation ten minutes twice daily.

Larry slipped my old white coat around my shoulders. Stepping out of the doors, the morning air hit our faces. It was still raining. I was surprised at the rain because I felt we had been at the hospital for days, not just ten hours.

Larry and I drove home in silence; his sunken eyes attested to his fatigue.

I wearily and slowly walked into the dining room in our home. I sat at the table, resting my head in my hands. My eyes glanced at a small heap near the hutch. A pair of green socks and new, brown "church shoes" was still drying where Dan had placed them the day before. It seemed an eternity since that joyful meal together, as well as the snuggling in the living room and the song service at church.

Amid the sad phone calls to grandparents and friends and the terror that struck my heart each time the phone rang, I ambled awkwardly around the house. I did not feel comfortable at home, and I did not feel comfortable at the hospital.

Larry's parents arrived the next day to help with our other children. My mother-in-law was a master at organizing the abundance of food that people brought.

Larry and I sat in the drab NICU waiting room once again. We were waiting with other hurting families to go in at the appointed time. No one dared be late. The door opened, and a nurse motioned for us to come in. Larry and I walked slowly by every bed to get to the one next to the window. The smell in the room was antiseptically nauseating. Some patients moaned. Some vomited. Some screamed. Some cursed. One could hear gurgling noises of people trying to breathe and the machines aiding them to do so. The beep of the heart monitors could be heard above all the other noises. Some patients had eyes open with a blank stare. Some had eyes rolled back. Some had no eye movement at all.

A retarded teenage boy in the bed next to Daniel's was thrashing about, having been pushed out of the emergency door of a school bus as a perverted prank.

We stood by Daniel's bed. This little one, looking exceedingly fragile, lay on a blanket of ice. The stiff body was beginning to curl up into a fetal position. Dan's pink rotund cheeks looked even more round and flushed with the white gauze surrounding his head. His chest heaved in labored breathing. A surgical cut in his throat called a tracheotomy was done the next day to aid his breathing.

Three days after the injury, I just knew the Lord would heal Dan. After all, it was Larry's birthday and it would be the absolutely perfect gift.

It was a cool Virginia autumn day with the sun beaming and a slight breeze. My heart was full of brightness as well when I anticipated our 2:00 p.m. visit with Daniel. I could picture in my heart Dan's sitting up, tubes gone, eyes open, and his wanting to go home.

I rehearsed how I would tell everyone about his healing.

The NICU door opened slowly to reveal the still-stiffened body next to the window.

How could God be so cruel? He had missed the perfect time to heal Daniel. Disappointed in my Heavenly Father, I fled to the waiting room. Larry stayed with Dan and patiently explained to his little "carbon copy" about the injury. Although he had no idea if Daniel could hear him, he reaffirmed to his son that Jesus was there with him even when we could not be.

Larry was told that Daniel had hovered close to death most of the day with his temperature ranging from 94 degrees to 105 degrees in one hour. His blood pressure and respiration were extremely poor, and the nurses had almost called us several times to come to the hospital.

As I slouched in grief on a sagging couch in the waiting room, a nurse came into the room where Larry had joined me. She inquired bluntly, "Have you ever considered donating Dan's kidneys?" My body nervously shook. How could she talk of dissecting my son? Words would not pass my lips, although I wanted to shout, "Shut up. Those kidneys were formed in my womb. They have worked very well for someone I love. I love his heart and his lungs and his brain and his fingers and his toes, and his kidneys. You can't have any of them."

The nurse's timing may not have been the best, but I am confident her motives were noble. Perhaps she had in mind another mother's little one who desperately needed the kidneys.

That night at church many gathered to pray instead of party. I played the piano as our loving congregation sang, "Does Jesus Care?" I questioned in my heart, "Does He care? Does He really? Then why didn't He heal Dan? It would be such a simple thing for Him to do." I remembered the prayer I had prayed two weeks earlier during the mission conference, "Lord, take my children and do anything you want in their lives."

After the singing I took my seat to listen to my husband preach. Clutching the pulpit, he looked so tired. But he preached with new authority.

Realizing again it was Larry's birthday, I prayed, "Lord, *I WILL NEVER* understand why you are letting my dear husband suffer so."

And in my heart, He seemed to say, "I understand, Jane."

The "*I WILL NEVER...*" Chapter 7

(Or, "*I WILL NEVER* believe God will not heal Daniel")

Three excited children had been preparing for Daddy's special day for several months. Knowing the Word of God hidden in his children's hearts reigned as a priority in Larry's life, the children had been memorizing scripture portions to recite to him. Becky complained often, "I know I make Daddy happy, but you can't wrap them verses up." Little did she realize that her dimpled face was all the wrapping her daddy needed.

With sagging spirits, we routinely went through the motions of living now that Daniel was in a coma. It was on particularly gloomy days that bubbly Becky seemed to echo from her playroom, "The Lord is my Shepherd." And during each long day, as the sought-for miracle did not come, the words resounded in my heart, "The Lord is my Shepherd." Oh, blessed truth.

I kept waiting for visits to the hospital to become easier. "After all," I reminded myself, "I'm new at this grieving business. Maybe people get used to it after a while." With empty assurances such as that, Larry took me up on the mountain behind the hospital after a difficult visit in NICU. The contrast between the fresh mountain air and the stale hospital aroma was striking. As we slowly walked to a lookout point, happy families with children walked in front of us. Nearby, several couples were holding hands. I resented such happiness, finding it astounding that anyone could be joyful when I hurt so deeply. Jealous and frustrated, I asked Larry to take me home.

Another week passed with no significant change in Daniel. Our despondency was tiring to our bodies and emotions.

My father-in-law accompanied me to the hospital. As we stood by Dan's bed, Daniel began strangling and gasping for air. The nurse quickly told us to leave. Larry's dad and I silently kept our vigil in the hall, trying not to imagine what was happening on the other side of the closed door. I thanked God that I had someone with me and asked Him for wisdom in breaking the fatal news to Larry once I got home. When we no longer could stand waiting in the hall, my father-in-law hesitantly tapped on the door. I stood behind him, hoping he could shield me from the news that Daniel had died. Opening the door, the nurse apologized, "Oh, come on in. I forgot to come get you after I suctioned Daniel's 'trach' out." Our wobbly legs hardly supported us as we went back in for a few remaining minutes.

Although the coma was a deep one, the nurses talked freely to Dan and encouraged us to do so. At each visit Larry patiently explained Dan's injury to him. Guilt overwhelmed me because I could not talk with ease. I had my one line

33

memorized; "Daniel, I love you, and I want you to get well and come back home." Then I began weeping and would leave.

Devastated by my growing guilt, I went to God in prayer. I was reminded of a Bible verse Daniel had been memorizing before he fell: "My sheep hear My voice," (John 10:27 KJV). God was using His Word to remind me that, although I was not loquacious, there was a Shepherd who promised His voice would be heard by His sheep - and lambs. With a soothing in my heart, I prayed, "Dearest Shepherd, I have a lamb that is hurting and needs to hear Your voice. Would You please talk to him for me?"

Peace flooded my soul.

Then I wondered if I should tell the Lord what to say. It did seem a bit presumptuous, but I had so many things I wanted to say to my boy. I decided that since Jesus could take all the time He wanted and could say anything He wanted, surely a "P.S. from Mother" would not be too out of place. And so I innocently prayed, "Father, you can tell him anything You want. But I have a few things I need You to pass on for me." Then added, "By the way, my broken lamb is the one over by the window, with the white gauze on his head and who is in a fetal position." And the Shepherd, who knows the hearts of Momma Sheep, did more than I dreamed.

Excited, I could picture this activity going on between Heaven and a little NICU room in the Roanoke Valley. I felt like an undercover agent who knew about secret communications no one else was privy to. Only the Shepherd knew - and a weary mother and a little lamb.

Larry compiled a "Diary of God's Grace" with various verses of scripture the Lord comforted us with daily. Each time Larry went in to see Daniel, he quoted the verse Dan had memorized for Larry's birthday but never got to recite:

God is our refuge and strength, abundantly available to help in tight places.

Psalm 46:1, *marginal reading*

The report that Dan had a slight flutter in his pupil made us euphoric. And when he moved his big toe as the nurse went through her daily routine of scraping her thumbnail firmly and quickly up his foot, we were elated beyond words. It was nearing Thanksgiving, and I concluded God had just been waiting until that special day to heal Daniel.

As others went to family homes and shared turkey and the fixings, we went to the hospital. Again, there was no healing; Dan merely moved his head from side to side. Part of his lung had collapsed because of pneumonia, and the coma was still deep. Larry again signed papers for a surgical incision into the stomach wall for insertion of a large tube to be used for feeding. The doctor explained, "The narrow tube down his nose is complicating his pneumonia. And he can get more nourishment through this larger tube. Besides, this is going to be a long haul, you know."

It would *not* be a long haul. God loved me, and He loved Larry, and He loved Daniel, and He had great power. I gritted my teeth, thrust my hands into my coat pockets, and said to myself, "*I WILL NEVER* believe He will not heal Daniel. There is no reason why He should not heal my son."

There was so little we could do for Dan; my excitement spilled all over the shoe store after the physical therapist requested some boots to hold Dan's pointed, rigid feet in a fixed position. The therapist hoped to alleviate shrinkage of his Achilles tendons. It was tricky to get those firmly-pointed-toward-the-end-of-the-bed feet into socks and boots. The dear little naked boy, dressed only in boots, looked a bit unusual, although he was the best-dressed one in the Intensive Care Unit since he had on more than anyone. The boots were short lived because of blisters, and the feet remained rigid, as did his right arm tucked under his chin in a tight fist.

On December 1st, Dan's eyes were slit open ever so slightly. Overjoyed, I lifted his eyelids and facetiously asked, "Daniel Bateman, you are in there after all, aren't you?" His eyes were again tightly shut when Larry visited in the evening.

Several days later Larry called the front desk of the hospital to inquire about something insignificant. The operator cautiously reported, "Rev. Bateman, I really believe you should talk to the NICU."

Now what?

Larry's face beamed as he screamed, "Jane, he opened his eyes! He stuck out his tongue!" Although it was December, I ran coatless and shoeless to each neighbor shouting, "He opened his eyes and stuck out his tongue." The neighborhood lit up long before Christmas.

And that night, I did something I had not been able to do for six weeks - I ate.

In the evening the deacons from our church joined their pastor as they went to the hospital to anoint Daniel with oil. Dan would neither open his eyes nor stick out his tongue for them, and although the coma seemed lessened only slightly, the faith and joy in our hearts knew no bounds.

I decided that since the Lord did not heal Dan on Larry's birthday or Thanksgiving, maybe He was just waiting for His own birthday.

A new form of therapy was begun. We loved it and called it "cuddling therapy." Larry and I took turns rocking Dan in a chair. It was indeed difficult to rearrange various tubes and to briefly disconnect others. It is hard to cuddle a totally rigid body, but we enjoyed those special times with him. As Larry held Dan, he prayed for him and talked soothingly to him. When I held him, I prayed, sang to him, and read favorite books. Neither of us was sure Dan heard us.

As the tracheotomy was "plugged" from time to time, Dan's lungs labored to get air through his mouth. Larry and I almost hyperventilated as our lungs worked in sympathy with Daniel's.

We never got used to the atmosphere in the ICU, nor did we get accustomed to being asked to leave because someone in a nearby bed had just "expired." I was startled, however, as I was met by a policeman standing by the door. He asked me for identification before I was allowed to enter the ICU. He explained he was stationed there to protect the patients inside. An angered relative of a patient, who had unsuccessfully tried to commit suicide, threatened to enter the hospital unit and "finish off the job." A policeman was standing guard inside the room while I visited. I was happy to make it a short visit.

Christmas was coming soon, and Dan smiled as if in anticipation. He smiled as he glanced at his beloved baseball glove. He smiled at his wrapped Christmas gift. And he smiled when Larry and I learned to feed him with a syringe inserted in his stomach tube. We all smiled when he ate a half a cup of ice cream by mouth.

Tinsel was draped around the heart monitors, and the NICU staff hoped to win the "best decorated department" award in the hospital. The sagging little tree cheered the place up not one bit. Festivity seemed out of place.

I tried to develop a larger "repertoire" of music because it seemed whenever I sang to Dan, the staff allowed me to stay longer. During a songfest, I held Dan in my lap, and he gently smiled at me through half-mast eyes.

A very loud, large man with delirium tremors from his activity in his mountain still heaved, swore, and yelled as I sang. He cursed the nurse because he could not vomit. The weary nurse glanced toward me and admonished, "Mrs. Bateman, sing louder." I bellowed Christmas carols as loudly as I could to four unconscious people, one semi-conscious little boy in my lap, and one gaggin', cussin' moonshiner.

Carrying Daniel back to his bed, I soothed his fuzzy head (the hair beginning to grow back), and I whispered, "Oh, Daniel, He did come as a baby. And there was great rejoicing. His mother loved Him, much like I love you. She cradled Him, much as I cradle you. She saw Him suffer, much as I see you suffer. And her heart was wrenched, much as mine is wrenched. But Dan, after He gave His life for us, He arose. What happy news. No wonder the angels sang at His birth. They knew the end of the story. I don't know the end of your story, sweetheart...."

Christmas arrived and left with nothing but sad memories. My parents saw Daniel for the first time since his injury and were grief-stricken as they remembered the bubbly little boy who had visited them earlier that summer. Dan beamed when they warily came into the room.

My daddy brought his ukulele and sang to Daniel. It was only much later that I realized how hard that was on Daddy.

Trying to motivate Daniel to talk, the staff suggested that we promise him that, if he talked, he could open his Christmas gift. Dan futilely attempted to say "Daddy." My lips, in sympathy, formed the word. Larry's body leaned forward, as if to put the word in his mouth. Exasperated, we opened his gifts for him. He grinned at the beloved G.I. Joe. It had been only about a month since we had bought the gifts on our autumn trip, but it seemed a lifetime had passed since then. My "little traveler," who had wanted to peek at the exciting boxes of toys in the car as we had traveled, laid back exhausted as we held up his gift.

The room was virtually empty because the staff attempted to let everyone who was able to go home for the holidays.

The bed by the window was still occupied.

Larry and I drove home in sleet and in silence.

I thought about my other two children. I hardly knew what they had received for Christmas. I thought about the Christmas dinner at the restaurant and the mountains surrounding the restaurant. And I thought about my plate resting with my food untouched.

I lay in bed, and I felt cold. It was the same kind of cold I felt when I lived with my grandparents as a little girl and felt homesick. It was neither cold feet, which I could warm against my husband, nor cold hands, which I could nestle under the covers. It was a chill in my heart.

Propped on one elbow, I observed my worn husband sleeping next to me. His countenance reminded me about a poem I had read. It described Dan and Larry perfectly:

> *Everything I found in him*
> *I found again in you.*
> *All the magic of a dream*
> *somehow twice come true,*
> *You're a darling duplicate,*
> *manly little lad,*

———

Of the great big fellow
*   that you proudly call your Dad.*

He is you, and you are he -
*   though you're Dad and son,*
In my heart your images
*   blend themselves in one,*
Love, when in a gracious mood,
*   sent your Dad, and then*
Nature, smiling roguishly, said
*   Here he is again!*

- Isabel Carolan

Remembering merrier Christmases, I prayed, "Father, thank you for sending your dear Son. Thank You that you know just how I feel tonight. Father, thinking of the glorious resurrection of your Son, I want you to know that *I WILL NEVER* believe you will not raise up my son as well. *I WILL NEVER* accept the fact that you will not heal him."

And in my heart, He seemed to say "Oh?"

The "*I WILL NEVER...*" Chapter 8

(Or, "*I WILL NEVER* get used to this")

"Ruling the roost" from his mute, horizontal position, Daniel supervised nurses with his skinny, left index finger, pointing out patients he felt were in need. An "O.K." sign that followed seemed to indicate his approval of their service.

Fifty-one days after his fall, Dan was moved to a private room. Unable to adjust the television, or ask for food, or turn over in bed, Daniel spent his spare time shredding his disposable diapers.

I was to relieve Larry after he spent the night with Dan. I felt nervous because I had not had to care for him alone. As I boarded the crowded elevator, I stared at the numbers on the wall, and my stomach got tighter per floor.

Arriving at Dan's room, I was overwhelmed when I saw Daniel surrounded by pajama-clad Larry and various medical staff. Desperation was written on Larry's face. My knees buckled somewhat as I overheard a nurse mumble, "Get a specialist."

I was too mortified to ask questions. I tried to ease my way on the periphery of it all.

A member of the medical staff spoke out of the corner of his mouth; "Daniel just did his own surgery. He yanked out the tube from his stomach. It was surgically sewn in and should have been surgically removed." I stood on tiptoe to see over the sea of white in front of me. In total contrast to the physicians, Dan's face radiated with success. Dan pointed to his mouth with obvious delight as if saying, "Please put food into this mouth."

Daniel was the only happy person in the room. No one seemed clear as to what to do. Should the tube be re-sewn into his stomach, or would he tear it out again? Should they chance feeding him by mouth, although he was so weak he could choke on his own saliva?

Maybe it was the confused, worried look of the professionals or the disheveled, disappointed look of my husband, but whatever it was that frightened me, I fled the room and vomited.

Larry sent me home.

Relieved and agitated at the same time, I drove home. I thought about the lines around Larry's eyes. They had hinted at his feelings: *I failed in my first night with him. It took me only 24 hours. How could I have let such a thing happen? We've fought so long to help him live, and I blew it...* I wondered if I should turn around and return to the hospital. Struggling with nausea, I continued on home.

The decision was made to bandage the new hole in Dan's stomach and hope he did not inhale food into his lungs as he ate by mouth. That could be fatal.

The brain damage had affected Dan's ability to discern when he was full, so he cried incessantly to be fed. The vicious cycle encircled the room hourly because the more he cried, the more frightened we became as Larry, so very cautiously, placed a tiny syringe into Dan's mouth to feed him. I balked at attempting it, and a nurse glibly handed me the syringe and admonished, "Listen, you're gonna have to do this sooner or later."

On New Year's Eve the thing we dreaded happened. Dan choked and vomited his food. A nurse and Larry literally threw him on his stomach so he would not aspirate. They whisked Dan to X-ray, and Larry called me. He uncharacteristically admitted, "Jane, I'm going under. This life-and-death situation with every mouthful is terrifying me. I can't take anymore."

Because it was humbling for me to admit I needed help, it was difficult for me to accept the offer of our church family to spend some nights with Dan. One family camped in Dan's room, and Dan enthusiastically rang a cowbell when he needed something (or when he did not need anything but excitement) assuring this loving couple, and most of the people on the hospital floor, a sleepless night.

I often thought, "Well, it's a new year, and I keep thinking I'll get used to all of this. But I believe *I WILL NEVER* get used to the screaming while the physical therapist pulls and bends stiffened limbs. *I WILL NEVER* get used to Dan's constant drooling and wailing."

There was little respite as we tucked pillows around the contorted body and put a neck brace on the limp neck and rolled Dan around the corridors in his wheelchair. With his "trach" scar healing, his long surgical scar peeping thorough his fuzzy head, his arm still tucked under his chin, he was indeed a sad sight. When we wheeled him to the playroom where other children were recovering from tonsillectomies and the like, they seemed fearful of Daniel. The mothers looked uncomfortable.

I leaned against the wall in the corridor just outside of Daniel's room when a smiling speech therapist summoned me into his room. I waited by his bed for my promised surprise. Slowly, Dan put his left hand to his mouth and used his fingers to help form the word. With great effort and shallow breathing, Daniel whispered, "Momma." My tears fell on his face as I leaned over and held this dear little boy. Never had that word sounded so sweet.

Gaining momentum, I called out spelling words, which Dan wrote with one finger on an erasable "magic slate." I gave out arithmetic problems on the same slate. No teacher ever reveled in her pupil's achievements such as I.

Putting the slate into his metal drawer, I said to myself, "We're on the road to recovery. *I WILL NEVER* again give in to discouragement."

Arriving at the hospital the next morning, I learned from a church member that Dan had fallen out of bed during the night. I quickly confronted a startled nurse; "How could that happen? That's how this whole thing started." My communication with her was too hysterical to be of much value, but I felt better after I had pled my cause.

Daniel's communication, on the other hand, was perplexing. At times, he communicated appropriately – at other times, he did not. We were catching on to his hand signals, but we wrongly interpreted the pulling off of nurse's hats and earrings as teasing.

In my best maternal fashion I concluded that Dan was sick of mushy milkshakes and applesauce. Because he had crunched ice for me, I knew he could chew, and I boldly gave him a small, hard sucker. I thought he would lick it and enjoy the taste. To my chagrin he bit the sucker in half and quickly devoured it. The next morning Dan could keep nothing on his stomach, and the staff assured me it was the flu going around the hospital. I was glad my "lollipop" secret was safe with Daniel.

The stretcher carried Dan to the rescue squad to go home the same way he had come to this hospital 81 days earlier. Tearful nurses bade farewell.

As we left, the doctor cautioned, "Remember, if you can't handle him at home, you can always bring him back."

And I pledged to myself, "*I WILL NEVER* give him over to professionals again. I'm his mother, and I will be the 'professional' in his life. This is one job *I WILL NEVER* fail at. The professionals WILL NEVER have him."

And, He who knows the future, seemed to ask, "Oh?"

The "*I WILL NEVER...*" Chapter 9

(Or, "*I WILL NEVER* send Daniel to camp")

The broad stripes and bright stars on the flag that had once flown over the Capitol Building in Washington, DC now proudly waved in Dan's newly painted red, white and blue room. When Dan entered his newly decorated room, the "home of the brave" seemed to take on a whole new meaning.

"Why on earth did we bring him home at lunch time?" I asked myself as I rustled up lunch. Mealtime was excruciating. Bad timing. As I looked into the cabinets, I comforted myself; "He's home now. Surely he doesn't need mush any longer. But I won't give him a sucker for dessert." Larry positioned Daniel in the reclining lawn chair we had brought into the kitchen.

Daniel vomited the entire meal. Panic-stricken, Larry thrust Dan forward while his frightened eyes glowered at me. As he carried his son into the bathroom, he sharply instructed, "Jane Lee, fix him something he can eat."

Frustration, fear, and failure swallowed me up. I sank onto the kitchen chair and prayed, "Lord, how could I fail in the first twenty minutes?"

I slept little that night. Larry had lovingly suggested I sleep on another floor of the house so that I would rest. My ears rested not a bit. I kept thinking I heard Daniel falling out of bed. Of course, the bunk beds had been dismantled the day after Daniel fell, but nonetheless I thought I heard him fall from his twin bed. It was just my overactive imagination.

The wearisome and long days began at 4:30 or 5 a.m. Daniel still required "intensive care," and we gave it without reservation. He took no naps to give us a break; his constant screaming to be fed and the need to puree the food proved overwhelming; the need to carry our partially paralyzed child around our two-story home was tiring, and the 10 p.m. bedtime was anxiously anticipated by a pair of drooping parents. I marvel at the strength God gave Larry and me. I had dropped to 87 pounds during Dan's lengthy hospitalization, and he was gaining weight faster than I since I had no time to eat and that was all he did.

It was a cold, misty January day as we excitedly drove to Easter Seals for physical therapy. Dan was uncooperative, screaming most of the time. I was embarrassed because I had never seen one of our children make such a public nuisance of himself. The frustrated therapist suggested a wheelchair race. One hand on one wheel was all Dan could manage due to the paralysis of his right arm and hand – and so his chair went around in circles. In anger, he beat his tight, right fist with his left hand.

As Dan wailed in the background, a well-meaning worker at Easter Seals suggested we sign Daniel up for Easter Seals Camp to be held in July. I was aghast. Dan was not a crippled child. This was temporary. How could the staff possibly imply that Dan would not be well by July? "*I WILL NEVER* believe this child will be like this in one month, much less in seven," I snapped. I ruminated in my thinking. "Thank you, but *I WILL NEVER* need your camp for crippled children."

Larry signed Daniel up for camp.

Why on earth was he doing that?

Slowly convinced that God had decided to use Larry and me in the healing process, Larry relentlessly exercised Dan's stiffened, sore, paralyzed limbs. I labored with his speech therapy. Dan's screams and questioning looks of how a loving Daddy could hurt his little boy often made me cry harder than Daniel. I frequently fled the house during those sessions as the mournful screams reverberated in my ears.

Hindsight has made us wonder if we should have actually been involved in these traumatic, painful exercises. We acted out of love, but we feared Daniel translated it differently.

One cold, dark morning our "Daniel Digital" clock sounded his alarm. After his usual "gourmet" breakfast at 5 a.m., I asked Daniel if he wanted to watch the farmer's report on television, the only thing on at that hour, or go back to bed. He chose instead to blow bubbles. This was an exercise we used in speech therapy since one needs breath control and tongue and lip movement to blow bubbles. As I pulled my robe around me and looked down at my dirty fuzzy slippers, I saw the tiny stream of bubbles hit the gold carpet. I sleepily remarked, "You know, Dan, I just bet we are the only people in the whole valley blowing bubbles at this hour."

In the evenings I held an ice cream cone just out of reach of Dan's tongue while he stretched his tongue to lick it. He reminded me of a frog zapping a fly for supper.

Dan's hard work was paying dividends, and by February, four months after he'd fallen, he could eat table foods and crawl on two knees and one hand. When he stood alone twelve seconds, father and son were ecstatic as they told me about it when I called from shopping.

A regal welcome awaited the pastor's son as he returned to church. Our dear flock had loved him and prayed for him as their very own. While Larry preached, I took all the children downstairs for a special story time. Before the story, we sang the song "Fairest Lord Jesus" from a large illustrated visual aid with magnificent, bright pictures of the Savior. The children wiggled with extra joy this morning.

That is, all except the little seven-year-old boy in the wheelchair.

Kneeling beside the wheelchair, I asked, "Daniel, can you tell Momma why you're crying?" His left hand slowly went to his lips to help form the words. Bathed heavily in raw emotion, Dan cried, "Momma, He was just like those pictures. He was so bright when I saw Him. And He talked to me..."

The halting, faltering words expressed vividly all I needed to hear. I recalled asking the dear Shepherd to talk to my lamb. And He had done so.

A bright and wonderful Companion had accompanied my "best little traveler" during the long coma. This Companion had heard a desperate mother's request. My baby even shared with me some of the Shepherd's words on their journey in the "valley of the shadow of death."

I kept those words in my heart and pondered them, as did another mother when her Son was on earth.

This Sunday afternoon I did not sit in the car in our driveway as usual and read the newspaper while Larry watched the children - (The car was the only quiet place I could find, but I needed to be close by for any emergency that might arise). *This* afternoon, I folded the paper in my lap.

Leaning back against the car seat, I reflected on the sacredness of the morning in children's church. I gazed at the snowcapped peaks and prayed, "Father, the days are so long. There's so little time to pray. But thank you for talking to my broken lamb during his comatose days. *I WILL NEVER* give up until he's walking, talking, and emotionally whole."

And, in my heart, the Shepherd seemed to whisper, "I love you, Momma Sheep!"

The "*I WILL NEVER...*" Chapter 10

(Or, "*I WILL NEVER* live through this")

I sat cross-legged on the floor, motioning for Daniel to come to me. Wobbly, but determined, he swung each leg just enough to make him mobile. When he reached me, we cried together and hugged so tightly I feared we might crush each other.

I dialed Larry's office, and winking at Dan, I soberly said to my husband on the phone, "Larry, you need to come home right away." I tried to sound solemn, but I could contain the joy no longer. I blurted loudly, "Larry, he walked! He walked." I called everyone I knew, and some I did not know, and even called the shoe store where I had purchased the boots for Daniel when he was in a coma.

Larry rushed home and recorded Dan's walking, just as we had done six years earlier when he walked the first time as a baby. Looking at those movies now, we see an incredibly unstable boy with his shirt wet from drooling and a right hand firmly knotted under his chin. But THAT day we only beheld the miracle.

Later that week, Dan used his left hand to pull his right fist slowly down from beneath his chin. He carefully placed the fist on the table. As we breathlessly watched, the tightened fist opened as a rosebud flowering forth. The concentration on our son's face and the trembling arm revealed how difficult this new feat was. I kissed each finger before the hand sprung closed. We celebrated with a candle in the hamburger that night.

Again, the camera was retrieved from the top of the closet. We joyfully explained to Dan how few children ever get to push their wheelchair back up the ramp at Easter Seals and say, "Thanks, but I don't need it anymore." But push it up the ramp he did - with a dejected, sad look on his face. Daniel reacted strangely in situations, and we could not explain his behavior.

Our greatest battle still centered on Dan's inability to know when he was full. He ate raw cake batter, grease, and any bits of food he found on the floor.

Eventually, we bought table and chairs with casters on them so we could scoot around the kitchen before Daniel tried to eat our food after inhaling his own. It reminded us of bumper cars at the amusement park. We became the fastest eaters in Virginia out of the need for survival because Dan stalked us while we ate. A typical meal was to pray (with our hands over our plate to protect our food), quickly consume our food, avoid any unnecessary conversation, and then leave the table. Took ten minutes at most.

We tried a new tactic of feeding Daniel early and putting him in his room so we could eat peacefully. If we could ignore the wails and the kicks on the door, we could almost digest our food.

Winter had seemed long.

The days, endless.

Although it had been only five months since Daniel had fallen, it seemed like five hundred years.

But as the jonquils began to bloom and sunny skies pushed away the gray ones, spring was indeed a welcome friend. Now glimpses of sunlight greeted us in our early morning hours.

Fourteen hours daily for months, I had tried to be the perfect nurse, perfect cook (and puree-er), perfect disciplinarian, perfect speech therapist, perfect school teacher, perfect hygienist, perfect occupational therapist, and perfect psychologist. In addition, I had endeavored to be the perfect wife, perfect lover, perfect pastor's wife, perfect mother to David and Becky, (trying in vain to play with them, go to PTA meetings, ball games), perfect laundress (keeping up with the mounds of dirty linens and clothing that Dan soiled daily), and perfect homemaker.

Sensing I was in desperate need of respite, my dear husband took Daniel to North Carolina to visit his parents. David and Becky went to West Virginia to be with my parents.

The house was hauntingly still.

Eerie.

Just God and me.

I felt choked by my new freedom.

I sat numbly on the couch, my insides still swirling on "automatic pilot." I had not realized how tired my body was. It felt heavy.

After the initial shock of my own company, I decided I needed to "plot my course," so as not to waste one moment of the week. I listed the luxuries I had missed the most over the past months: eating, sleeping, taking a bath, praying, reading the Bible, going to church, and shopping. I lifted my weary body from the couch and took a twenty-minute bath. Then I decided to do something terribly risqué - I went to a restaurant and had waffles for supper, slowly savoring every bite. No bumper cars there.

I went to every church service I could find that week, spent precious times praying and devouring the Word of God, shopped in every store in the Valley, called every friend I had not talked to in months, ate every meal out, slept late every morning, and tried to clean house a bit.

A week alone was all I needed.

David and Becky came home first and went with me to the airport. I cried as the gentle man and the crippled boy got off the plane. As the tired man pushed the boy in an airport wheelchair, I wanted to yell, "Hey, everyone. See those two - the man and the boy who look so much alike - they belong to me. And I get to care for the boy - and the man takes care of the boy and me and two other incredible children. We all love each other, and we aren't any good at being separated."

As we drove home with the car windows down, fresh air beat our faces. I glanced in the back seat at three marvelous children. I looked over at the handsome man driving the car.

I smiled and prayed, "Father, it's so wonderful to be together again. *I WILL NEVER* allow us to be separated for such a long time again."

And in my heart He seemed to say, "Oh?"

The "*I WILL NEVER...*" Chapter 11

(Or, "*I WILL NEVER* go out in public again")

Awkward children, some seeing Dan for the first time since his injury, bustled into the living room to help celebrate his eighth birthday. Dan screamed when he lost the game of "clothespins-into-the-bottle;" he screamed when the winner got her candy bar; he screamed when he lost "Pin the tail on the donkey." He screamed when everyone left. He wanted to eat his entire cake by himself.

It was horrible from start to finish.

Later I tucked Daniel into bed and stayed awhile in his room. He slept soundly, and I wistfully remembered that May Day eight years earlier. He had been a perfect tiny specimen. He had learned to walk and talk with such ease. The second time around had been so much more difficult. I collapsed in bed after one last look at my boy.

The physical progress was wonderful in direct contrast to the emotional upheavals. The sudden screams and thunderous crying were unpredictable. It was as if we were living with a "time bomb" because we never knew when he was going to "blow."

He was becoming stronger, and there were subtle signs of aggression as well as threats to hit, bite, or kick someone. Family was not exempt.

Daniel was desperately lonely to be with other children, and he accompanied me into the "Bluebird" room to pick up Becky at her nursery school. His behavior was obnoxious, trying to tickle or pinch the children, and parents became uneasy as this crippled, drooling boy approached. I was afraid he would injure one of the little ones and tried leaving him in the car just long enough for me to run into the building, grab Becky's hand, and run back to the car. On several occasions, he escaped from the car. The other times, he laid on the horn.

These embarrassing displays caused both Becky and me to hate those two days a week.

One day Becky ran to us, proudly holding her fragile, priceless handwork, and Dan jealously tried to destroy it. I'm not sure who was sadder — Becky or her mother.

I had scheduled an activity for our hyperactive, bored son for every moment of the day. He learned to fold clothes with one hand, help make beds, help me empty the dishwasher, push the vacuum, scour the sink, and now he was going to re-learn how to tie a shoe. Becky was included in the lesson since she had not yet mastered the fine art of shoe tying. I was not certain how to teach someone to tie a shoe with one hand, but I was going to give it all I had. I got Larry's large tennis shoes and gave one to each child.

Daniel and I concentrated and worked together for a long time. We almost missed a small feminine voice proudly announcing, "Look Mommy and Daniel, I tied it."

Utterly humiliated, Dan tried to hurl the large shoe at his sister. Becky's pride fading, she left the room while I held Dan and the shoe. Daniel sobbed on my shoulder. His head had known how to tie, but his hands would not cooperate. His four-year-old sister had succeeded where he had failed.

Because of Dan's unsociable behavior with others, we had the same discussion each time we drove to speech therapy at the Roanoke Valley Speech and Hearing Clinic. "Dan, should you tease any of the other children in the waiting room? Should you scream and kick when you cannot pronounce a new word in therapy? Let's talk about good behavior..." The lessons *discussed* in the car were *left* in the car when we entered the building.

At the speech and hearing clinic, a little deaf patient was having his birthday party. Driving into the city, I prayed, "Oh, God, please don't let Dan hurt anyone."

The room was festive with balloons and a tall three-tiered cake. All 100 guests had speech and/or hearing problems, but only one had a severe hunger problem. As Dan and I entered the crowded room, we joined the others admiring the large birthday cake, which stood as high as the birthday boy himself. Dan bolted from me, and with his index finger, scraped sugary white icing from the top to the bottom of the cake and plunged it into his mouth. The entire horrifying incident took place in two seconds.

There were gasps. I heard people murmur, "Oh, no - he's ruined it."

Dan and I were asked to wait in another room until the party began. I was almost hoping they would forget to come get us once the party got under way, but we were ushered out for the rousing Happy Birthday song. At the end of the song quiet reigned, and Daniel gustily sang, "Amen, again." Every eye glared in our direction.

Although I kept Daniel occupied during most of the day, terror struck my heart as the school bus stopped in front of our house. Daniel wanted to greet the children. I tried closing the curtains, but his internal alarm system seemed to signal 3:10 p.m. I accompanied him to the stop, and he greeted each friend with, "Hi, wanna play?" Each had his reason for being "busy," and Dan leaned on my shoulder and wailed as we walked into the house together.

I could shelter him no longer. "Perhaps I am over-protecting him. Maybe I should do as the professionals prescribed and treat him as a normal child. Maybe he won't really hurt the children. It is not fair to keep him in our yard all the time and make David stay home and play with him," I reassured myself.

The next day the familiar squeaky bus door opened and children poured out in their usual bustling fashion. Daniel awkwardly stood by as they talked and laughed among themselves. Hesitantly, I announced, "Dan, you may go to someone's yard and play." The children stared at me. Dan looked at me in disbelief but proudly cantered two doors down from our house. He looked like a caged bird suddenly free. In trepidation, I went into our house. I sat on our sofa, leaning forward, waiting for the explosion.

It took less than two minutes.

Hearing screams, I dashed to the next yard where painters were stirring and applying luscious white paint to a house. With bright red blood gushing from an unknown part of his anatomy, Dan was blindly, unsteadily running close to the paint buckets. The startled painters tried to assist Dan and protect their white paint from instantly turning pink.

Leading my totally out-of-control child into the house, I tried to narrow down the blood spouting like a volcano. The phone interrupted my first-aid attempts as our neighbor reported the incident. Dan had triumphantly knocked on their storm door, anxious to tell them of his new freedom to play. When no one answered, he thrust his fist through the window.

After bandaging Daniel, I tried to calm down. I was tempted to call the professionals to explain their prescription of freedom lasted two minutes.

Wiping the blood off the kitchen floor, I mumbled, "Counselors. What do they know? They sit with books in paneled offices. They do not live here day in and day out. *I WILL NEVER* depend on their so-called wisdom again."

And, in my heart, He seemed to say, "Oh?"

The "*I WILL NEVER...*" Chapter 12

(Or, "*I WILL NEVER* explain this one to Larry")

Blowing Cheerios off of my own nose and walking blindfolded and barefoot across the floor searching with our feet for scotch tape on the carpet were not the time fillers I had hoped they would be. Sitting on the gold carpet and picking up the stubborn pieces of scotch tape clinging to the rug, I leaned back against the wall and sighed, "Oh, Father, I am so tired of trying to be a full-time playmate to someone with a two-minute attention span. Please send help."

And God did just that.

A relative located a visiting "mom's helper" who agreed to give me a respite twice a week for several hours. I looked forward to her coming as much as I, as a child, had anticipated the final bell at school before summer vacation. This lovely black lady had not worked for us long when I bounced through the front door from my shopping. Her eyes were wide as she greeted me at the door and blurted out breathlessly,

"Mrs. Bateman, I just turned my back a split second, and Danny was gone. I ran up and down your street screaming his name. I sent little Becky to your neighbors' yards looking." She took a deep breath, and her voice elevated several octaves as she continued, "I called my husband at work. Yes, I did. I said, 'I lost Danny. I just lost him.' And my husband said not to worry. Well, I hung up the phone and went into the kitchen, heading for your back door. And what do you suppose I found? This here crippled boy standing up on a chair eating the chocolate cake I had hidden on top of the refrigerator. He was stuffing his mouth with that one good hand. I think he had gone out the front door, and when he heard me screaming, he slipped around to the back door and has been feasting while this little girl and me have been scared to death."

Anxious to leave, she did not tarry for any sympathy.

The next week we had a new "mom's helper" sent from the agency, and upon my return home this large maternal lady greeted me at the door. She grabbed her purse and crisply yelled over her shoulder, "Lady, I can't take this. You can have your kids. I quit!"

So much for that avenue of help.

The spring breezes through the open windows smelled like a field of honeysuckle. The dejected eight-year old who had lived for this Little League season stood at the open windows and waved as the haunting sounds of "batter up" and "Run! Run!" burst in. His waving seemed symbolic to a world passing him by. The wailing and waving continued each evening for the entire season. I stood at the door and pleaded with God to send rain so that the cheers would be mute for just one evening. To my dismay, however, it was one of the driest summers in Virginia history. As David donned his uniform, the baseball cap shaded not a bit the deep conflict of playing while his brother could not.

The peaceful calm of the morning was unusually welcomed. The quiet seemed as warm as the summer sunshine, and Daniel and I ventured out into the sun for a picnic. Our little tree did not offer much shade, and the red Virginia clay was not yielding a lot of grass, but peanut butter sandwiches never tasted so good.

Golden silence permeated our souls when Dan cleared the peanut butter from the roof of his mouth and asked, "Mom, could I just sit on my bicycle?" I took my sunglasses off to get a clearer view of this question and replied, "Oh, Daniel, I don't think that's a good idea. You are heavier now, and I am not sure I could steady you while you sit on it. Why don't I go in and get some bubbles to blow...we could blow the giant bubbles and see if they'll reach the mountains." My son insisted, "But, Mom, you wouldn't have to hold me up a lot. I can put my left leg down on the ground. I just wanna do it so bad. Please, Mom?" I brushed the crumbs off of our tattered blanket, and with uncertainty reeling in my voice, I explained, "Well, alright. But you must listen to what I say. And you must not resist my help when I try to steady you. And we'll keep the kickstand down too. Got it, Mr. Bateman?" With a gleam in his eyes, Dan crawled off the blanket, nibbling on forbidden crumbs left behind.

The utility room, dark and musty, took on the air of Christmas as I revealed the dusty red bike to a smiling boy. The sunshine made it look "redder" said Daniel, and he jumped for joy next to his beloved bike on which he had once traveled many miles around the neighborhood. I helped Dan straddle the two-wheeler and gently opened his fisted right hand, conforming it around the handlebar. I knew the hand was there to stay until we peeled it off, finger by finger. I stationed his lame right leg on the pedal so he could balance himself with his left leg.

Turning his head to check my position, my son directed me, "Momma, I'm O.K. I can balance myself. You can let go." Cautiously, I lifted my hands away for a few seconds...I thought. As Dan sped off in a cloud of dust and my whole life passed before my eyes, I warned myself, *"I WILL NEVER* explain this to Larry."

Going at full throttle and unable to use the hand brakes, Daniel stayed within the confines of our yard only because he knew I was prepared to lie down in the driveway to block his exit to the street.

I have an idea a weary angel somehow halted the bike as Dan victoriously chimed, "See, Mom, I knew I could do it. I just knew it."

It was awfully difficult to be upset with someone with so much "drive."

My heart had scarcely returned to its normal beat when Larry came home from work. Dan's excitement spilled all over the foyer as he met his dad and breathlessly mumbled, "I got a real surprise for you." Larry glanced his eyes in my direction wanting more information. I managed a sick smile. In duck-like fashion the family waddled behind Dan to the backyard.

Larry suspiciously viewed the bicycle and, in his best paternal *"I-mean-this"* voice, announced, "Absolutely not!"

Larry's resistance began to weaken after seeing his son's obvious delight. Feeling partially responsible for Daniel's previous escapade, I laid down firm ground rules (as if he would heed them).

Larry shifted nervously, and his eyes looked mortified as Dan proudly mounted his vehicle. Larry sternly interrogated me, "Jane Lee, he has no helmet. Suppose he hits his head? Suppose he rides faster than I can run to stop him? Jane Lee, how could you have let him do this?" He did not wait for answers. Surrounded by jubilant friends, neighbors, and a jogging Daddy, Dan soared down the street while I recorded it. It went well.

As the neighbors went home and I looked at our boy's merry triumphant face, I vowed, "*I WILL NEVER* overprotect him again. *I WILL NEVER* again cradle him so closely."

And He, who understands the balance of protection and freedom for His children, seemed to say in my heart, "Oh?"

The "*I WILL NEVER...*" Chapter 13

(Or, "*I WILL NEVER* forget the Bicentennial")

The clock announced we were late. I grabbed some bedroom slippers, our three children, and whizzed through the narrow roads to pick up three more children in our carpool. Our car fairly bulged, as we seemed to inch toward the school. The empty parking lot silently signaled we were late, and the children dashed down the long walk into the building. I sighed with relief and glanced into the rearview mirror before leaving. To my utter horror, Daniel Bateman was not in the car.

My slippers flapping against my heels and my heart racing, I ran down the long walk as Becky vainly tried to keep up with me. Reaching Dan's old classroom, my heart shattered. He was clinging to the desk he had once occupied before his injury. The stunned new resident of the desk stood by with a "squatter's rights" assurance on his face. Daniel laid his head on the desk and moaned, "This is my desk, and you can't sit here. I sit here. Oh, please, let me stay..."

The pleading cries echoed down the halls, and curious teachers, students, parents, and principals gathered. I tried to reason with Dan, but he wept bitterly. I tried to be firm, but he became hysterical. In desperation the teacher and I twisted and tugged his body, which was firmly glued to the desk. Because his feet were wrapped around the legs of the desk, we pulled both Dan and the desk into the hall. Someone helped me peel Daniel out of the desk and assisted me as I supported Dan's now limp frame to the car, his eyes closed in utter grief.

We both cried all the way home. I silently prayed, "Father, don't you see how awful this hurts?" I knew He understood. There have been times I have clung to forbidden territory, thinking I belonged, and He has had to tug, pry, and pull me out, His heart breaking all the while.

Once home, Daniel seemed to be soothed with a bowl of applesauce. I sat close by on our deck and thought about the struggles of the morning. I thought about the fine line that exists between dependence and independence. Dan had so longed for independence, and yet, it kept slipping away from him.

After the school bells rang for the last day of school, barefoot children took on a festive aura as independence and jubilation spilled throughout the neighborhood. The entire country took on the merriment of a giant birthday party. The Bicentennial celebration permeated every area of the nation. And this joyfulness wormed its way into the Roanoke Valley.

Before firecrackers pierced the night and fireworks adorned the heavens, the afternoon of July 4 was spent with our beloved church people at a member's rural home.

Canvas tents and awnings rented from a funeral home protected the Southern specialties spilling over on long tables. Dan went from table to table sampling each delicacy long before it was "eatin' time." His never knowing when he was full made social functions even more uncomfortable.

He was like an over-sized toddler trying to keep up with the other children. He stood at the bottom of the tall, swaying, suspended bridge and watched the others carefully slither across. He wept as he watched. He tried to play in ball games, but he could not hit the ball. And he wept. He tried to pet the cows behind the fence, but his balance gave way, and he hit the electrical barricade. And he wept. Although everyone tried to include Daniel, he just did not fit. Dan and I rode in a crowded pickup truck back to the main road and drove home in the early afternoon. Watching the mammoth celebrations on television together, I indulged in a genuine pity-party for Jane.

The whole month of July seemed to mock me. Camp Easter Seals was lurking in the shadows, and I was bitterly disappointed that we did indeed still have a crippled child. Winding through the Virginia hills, the hour-long ride to the camp was a quiet one. Apprehension dulled any attempts at conversation. It is one thing to take a normal, healthy child to camp and quite another to entrust one with varied needs to other people.

Hugs and kisses and tears over, we trekked back to the car. I smiled faintly, remembering our insistence that Daniel be given a bottom bunk, although he was one of the more mobile campers. I glanced over my shoulder for one last peek and saw Dan joyfully marching toward the specially equipped swings for handicapped children. He looked euphoric. Independent. He fit.

Larry and I spent two days at the beach alone, trying to get reacquainted. We were both so tired physically and so drained emotionally that we behaved as strangers. We had vowed not to talk about Daniel, but because our world was so narrow, we stuttered at any dialogue.

In August our silver station wagon wound through tall pine tress with the sign, "Camp Easter Seals" peering through to welcome us. All of us jumped from the car at the same time in excitement. A battle-worn, deliriously happy little boy with blood oozing from his nose and mouth stumbled toward us. We learned the good news first - the daily intensive speech therapy had paid huge dividends; he was more independent in caring for himself, and he was a terrific swimmer, even conquering the coveted "Tadpole" award. The bad news was he had been bitterly homesick the entire three weeks, had huge blisters on his feet from new corrective shoes, and had fallen often, causing the bleeding; and had tried to smack his speech therapist. The staff, battle-worn and weary in their own right, seemed deliriously happy to see us as well. We got the hint that Dan, although one of the more mobile children, presented more problems than all the other campers combined.

Happy to be together again, the Bateman family loaded the mounds of dirty clothes and two tiny earplugs that had "Dan B." written minutely on them, along with disintegrating priceless camp crafts, into the car. Dan taught us camp songs, and we laughed as Becky tried to master them.

The counselor's comment was gnawing in the back of my mind; *He tried to hit me*. I could hardly believe such a thing. Surely, she just did not know how to handle him.

I declared to myself, *"I WILL NEVER allow Daniel to ever hurt another person. I will see to that."*

And He who knows the future seemed to say in my heart, "Oh?"

The "*I WILL NEVER...*" Chapter 14

(Or, "*I WILL NEVER* lock anyone up")

Boundless energy of an eight year old raged within an old man's body. Dan's sharp mind remembered when his body was his servant, and now he was its slave.

The summer brought increasing frustration for the whole family. Children played everywhere, and Daniel hovered agonizingly close, yet excruciatingly distant. Longing to be in the mainstream, he was, nonetheless, always teetering on the periphery.

Threatening behavior escalated in intensity. Our son's frustration and anger were channeled into one good fist, sharp teeth, and one good leg. He hurled objects. He beat himself. These unexpected outbursts erupted with startling inconsistencies, and Larry summarized Dan's emotions to someone as, "The only predictable thing about Dan is his unpredictability."

"Man, I'd have popped him on his bottom," some advised. We did. Some suggested we withhold the excessive food he craved. We did. Some hinted we curtail privileges.

Daniel did not enjoy that many privileges (we were more into survival than privileges), but we curtailed what we could.

How does one discipline a child when distinguishing between willful disobedience and outbursts that are rooted in brain damage? How does one discipline when one knows that outbursts cannot be overlooked, but one is unsure of the child's ability to control it?

We had no idea.

After a week when Daniel hit a very pregnant lady, busted my lip, bruised David's eye, and dumped a glass of milk on the head of a brave church member who offered to stay with him for an hour, we knew we desperately needed help.

But whom does one tell?

I nervously entered the small office at the Child Development Center. My green blouse was wet from fear, and my hair clung to my forehead. I flipped through a magazine, thinking perhaps I should leave, when a grandmotherly sort of lady greeted me. I dropped the magazine and anxiously followed her to her office. I had never opened up to anyone for two reasons: one, I had no time to talk with anyone, and two, it was humiliating to admit defeat.

As the sweet lady probed with leading questions, bottled up information spewed from me as a carbonated drink does from a shaken bottle. I was uncorked, and it felt delicious.

After I eventually fizzled out, I anticipated her standard reply: "Mrs. Bateman, surely it's not that bad. No one could live like you have described. You just need to be patient..." I leaned forward and put my chin on my hands as she softly drawled, "Mrs. Bateman, it sounds terrible. I don't see how y'all have lasted this long. You *must* get help." I felt warm. Cared about. Understood. I wallowed in her compassion and

70

had an urge to go around her desk and hug her tightly. After I set up another appointment, I waltzed from her office.

I drove home with a new gleam in my eye. The mountains took on a "from whence cometh my help" kind of appearance.

Larry and I met weekly with a child psychologist at the center to get hints on discipline. Some hints were helpful - some not. Hint one: Lock Daniel in his room when he acts out. I had several problems with hint one. I was not sure I could lock any child anywhere, and Daniel's door had no lock even if I had wanted to. I remembered there had been twenty-minute tug-of-war confrontations when I had managed to drag Dan to his room and held his door closed while he pounded on his window until I knew it would shatter. So, hint one seemed unfeasible.

Hint two: If Daniel was dangerous and I could not get him into his room - (I weighed 87 pounds, but Daniel's 70 pounds and "super-human" strength prevailed when he got angry), I should lock *myself* in my room for safety. That would not work because I knew he could leave the house while Mom cowered in her hideaway.

Hint three: Put stars on a chart every hour when there was no acting out. We tried this for weeks and there was little success and few stars. Finally, Dan complained, "I think this star stuff is silly."

We eventually tried herding Daniel into his room, tying his doorknob to ours and praying that his window resisted the pounding.

We were eager students desperately cramming to learn all we could in order to control this complicated person living with us.

71

But on Sundays our defeat was evident as the Pastor preached with bruises here and there, and the pianist had bleeding, raw knuckles.

I sat in the blue high-backed chair in our living room. Thinking about the frequent screams wafting out of our open windows to the homes of neighbors, I complained to God. After pouring a glass of iced tea, I settled once again in the chair. Down the hall Daniel was bellowing and pounding on his window. "I wonder what the neighbors think?" I mused. Then I prayed, "Father, *I WILL NEVER* give up on this discipline problem. I will learn how to manage my own precious son again."

And He, who knows how to mete out the right discipline at the right time for His children, seemed to ask in my heart, "Oh?"

The "*I WILL NEVER...*" Chapter 15

(Or, "*I WILL NEVER* get used to the principal's office")

"If only Dan could start school in the fall, he'll calm down." I simplistically comforted myself.

And start school he did.

A local elementary school designed a room for him and other learning-disabled children. A large janitor's closet was cleaned out, spruced up, and Dan settled in for one hour a day with his own private tutor.

He learned quickly, but as had been the case all along, his short attention span and aggression were the major problems. He earned an ice cream cone from the cafeteria if he went the whole hour with no problem.

After several months the school attempted to mainstream Dan into a regular second-grade classroom for math only. Before Daniel entered the classroom, the guidance counselor explained Dan's paralysis, drooling, and speech problems to the children. The first day Dan made a joke, and when everyone laughed on cue, he bolted out of the room. The second day he left because he was bored. He later stabbed the teacher with scissors.

By November the weary teachers were not able to cope. Phone calls were more frequent to pick Daniel up before his hour had expired. On one occasion the teacher, in desperation, sent Dan to the principal's office. Daniel put his good arm into a huge aquarium, attempting to overturn it. The office would have been flooded had not the principal restrained him. Having been summoned, I arrived to find a wet principal, a soggy, howling Daniel, and a few nervous fish.

In the afternoon Becky and I played Chinese checkers with Daniel. Because Becky jumped his marble and took it, Dan stuffed a handful of marbles in his mouth, attempting to swallow them. The remaining marbles he hurled at close range at his baby sister.

Larry came home early that day.

We knew time was running out. It was only a matter of days before we were called into the principal's office. I was surprised to discover that one never outgrows the trepidations that visit brings.

The aquarium gurgled as Larry and I sat in a circle with several school administrators and Dan's ever-patient teacher. The principal introduced us.

These educators sugarcoated the message so it would be palatable: Daniel did not fit. He was too disruptive for even the hour he was allowed to come. They shared pamphlets of expensive private schools in Northern Virginia, close to Washington, DC. I set my maternal jaw. *I WILL NEVER have him four hours away from us in some school.*

Some well-meaning soul even suggested military school. Considering the irony of that suggestion, I chuckled to myself that Daniel, unfortunately, did enjoy combat.

Problems were surfacing everywhere. School. Home. Speech therapy. Church. There was no demilitarized zone.

The psychologist suggested that since I was being bitten and pinched during church, it made more sense to let Dan tell me when he had had enough and leave. I felt as if I was abdicating, but I decided it was easier to switch than fight. We usually lasted through the song service and sometimes through his Daddy's morning announcements. Dan often obnoxiously responded verbally to his Daddy during these announcement times. I described the embarrassing scenes to another psychologist, and he cracked, "I thought everyone acted like that in a Baptist church."

I let my guard down a bit as we sailed along in our little Volkswagen bug en route to speech therapy, and Daniel reached between the seats and yanked the emergency brake up. The little beetle abruptly jerked, and Becky was flung forward from the back seat. To this day, I cannot tolerate anyone driving with a hand resting on the emergency brake.

I held Becky in my lap during Dan's speech therapy, and she rested her head against my shoulder. We were both uninjured, but it felt good to snuggle. Daniel approached me in the waiting room and asked, "Mom, can we stop for a treat on the way home?" Remembering my barren wallet, I knew I had to present my case cautiously. I intended to say, "Honey, I don't have money with me, but we have some pudding at home."

But after hearing only the first part of my response, Dan grabbed me in a headlock, and I fell to my knees. Mothers in the waiting room tried to assist me. I could hear one use the sweet approach, "Sweetie, let's not pull mother's hair." Another took a more direct approach when she pulled Daniel, who in turn pulled my hair in a hairy chain-reaction. My eyes stared at the carpet. I could have swept the rug with my eyelashes until Daniel released me. I dreaded facing this waiting room full of anxious-to-help people and was embarrassed by the whole ugly scene.

When we finally arrived home, I rubbed my sore head and knees and announced to Daniel that he had no chance at pudding.

"Dr. Jekyll" surfaced after our "Mr. Hyde" day, and Becky and Daniel decided to play church. Dan was the minister, Becky made up the choir, and I assisted as the deacon who made sure the preacher did not punch the choir out.

Our service went well, with a fine sermon from Preacher Dan. The choir sang with extra gusto, and I thought I "deacked" especially well since no one had to be ex-communicated from the service.

Becky sidled up to me and whispered, "I want to go to Heaven someday to be with Jesus. Tell me how." I took her into my arms, but it was Dan who began to speak. In his halting, thick speech, he began, "Becky, do you know God loves you so much?" Her brown eyes sparkled more than usual at such good news. Dan continued, "And Becky, did you know the Bible says 'all have sinned' (Romans 3:23 KJV) and that means you and me?" Becky looked at me to check out the theology of that accusation. I explained what sin was, and her saddened expression revealed her convicted heart. Dan asked, "Guess what - God loves you so much He didn't wanna punish you, so He punished Jesus instead. He was perfect and could die for our sins. And after He died, He arose. He wants to take away your sin, but you have to ask Him. You wanna ask Him, huh?"

After I read some verses from the Bible so Becky would understand God Himself was the author of this Good News, not her brother or mother, we knelt together. As we huddled on the green carpet in the playroom, the little girl simply invited Jesus to be her Savior. While she prayed, I kept one eye open lest Dan smack her since I am sure that is not what is meant by aggressive evangelism.

Daniel, Becky, and I hugged and kissed and rejoiced with the angels in heaven. What a priceless privilege to introduce our three children to the One who means more to their parents than life itself.

As I wearily lay down that night, I mused about the full day and the diverse behavior in it. "*I WILL NEVER* understand this baffling behavior, but *I WILL NEVER* move to another city to get help. Surely that could never be God's will for us."

And He who beholds diverse behavior in His own children seemed to ask in my heart, "Oh?"

The "*I WILL NEVER...*" Chapter 16

(Or, "*I WILL NEVER* move to Illinois")

One year had passed since Daniel's injury.

One year.

It was a merciful blur, and yet painfully clear.

We had come so far. But we had not come far enough.

Larry persistently contacted Christian schools for the handicapped all over the country. Each response began with, "We are sorry..." Dan did not fit. Either the school was for retarded children (and Daniel was not retarded), or they did not service aggressive children, or did not offer speech or physical therapy. It was uncanny how Dan had either too many or too few handicaps to qualify.

After months of praying, searching, and watching our volatile situation simmer and bubble, good news was placed in our mailbox. Larry excitedly read to me the letter from a Christian school for children with special needs willing to accept Daniel. I yelled on the inside, "There is help. There is hope. No longer will we live in combative limbo." I squealed, "Larry, where is this marvelous place?" He sat down on the edge of the sofa before speaking. "Jane Lee, it's in Illinois."

Illinois? I parted my lips to reveal my teeth, hoping the expression resembled a smile. Silently I jet-streamed to the Lord, "Didn't you hear me when we left Illinois before and I said *I WOULD NEVER* return there?" And He seemed to say, "Yes, I did." Not to be outdone by Sovereignty, I complained, "With all the world at your disposal, I don't see why you couldn't arrange help closer to home."

With deep conflict raging in my heart, I slowly descended the steps to our family room. A fire blazed in the fireplace, and I pulled my sweater tightly around me. I snuggled into the large green and red plaid chair next to the window and watched snow just beginning to coat the red clay and bits of grass.

"Father," I stammered, "I am willing to go anywhere you send me. But, Lord, our parents are only a few hours away. Neither Larry nor I have siblings to fill in the gap. There are no other grandchildren for them to enjoy. Please, Lord, please don't send us far away to the Midwest."

My neck suddenly snapped backwards over the chair. Dan had quietly sneaked down the steps and hid behind the chair. He grabbed my hair and pulled it, bending my head and neck backward over the top of the large chair. Because my air supply was being cut off, I could not yell for help. I gasped in a whisper, "Larry, come help. Larry, I need you." I pled with Daniel, but he only tightened his grip, causing excruciating pain and making me all the more immobile. It was not possible to reach around the big, overstuffed chair to grab Daniel's arms, nor could I pry his fingers off my hair. Eventually, sensing something was wrong, Larry bounded down the steps barely touching them. Larry restrained Dan tightly on the floor while I fled from the room screaming, "I can't stand this another minute. I'm going crazy. Larry, you've got to get us help!"

Suddenly, the distance we needed to travel to get help seemed trivial.

I flew to Chicago, toured the magnificent facility, and met with the principal. After we discussed policies, he suggested we walk across the path to view the dormitories. I squirmed nervously, "Oh, thank you, but I do not need to see those. *I WILL NEVER* allow Daniel to live outside our home. We will move here, and he will be a day student." The kind principal seemed perplexed that one would fly so far and yet not cross a small path to see the entire school. Adamantly, I refused. The thought of Dan's living in a dormitory nauseated me. He was our child, and we would raise him.

As I departed through the mounds of snow heaped beside the narrow school exit, I was beyond weary. I prayed silently, "Thank You for this wonderful place. It is perfect for Dan but I WILL *NEVER* have him in any dormitory. NEVER!"

And in my heart, He seemed to say, "Oh?"

The "*I WILL NEVER...*" Chapter 17

(Or, "*I WILL NEVER* doubt God's goodness")

Visions of Illinois cornfields danced in our heads as we went through the motions of our last Christmas in Virginia. The simple Christmas play at church had a young crippled shepherd. Although the towel headdress and long flannel bathrobe covered most of his body, the dimples gave him away. A halo could have easily accompanied the saintly gaze, until he abruptly became violent and was pulled behind the sheeted curtains.

Christmas Eve, Dan tried to hurl the television set at me as well as my parents. Mom and Dad had brought my grandmother from West Virginia to visit for the holidays. My grandmother died that night while visiting other family in the area. Christmas memories such as those are anxiously forgotten. Other memories are not so easily severed.

Pastor Larry's eyes skimmed the room and dared not rest on any one person in the congregation. His voice was taut, firm. He told this "flock" of his deep love for them and his joy at having been able to minister with them. The tight voice loosened and cracked as he said, "It is with deep regret that I must tender my resignation..." And it was with deep relief that he closed with prayer, so that all of the congregation could shut moist eyes.

The next morning, I reluctantly folded small shirts and warm sweaters and nestled them in the suitcase. Although I knew we would be joining Daniel soon in Illinois, it was difficult to let him go so far.

Dan's happy face beamed, and Larry's was stoic as the station wagon slowly pulled out of the driveway and headed west. I wore a synthetic smile and said all the things mothers are supposed to say – be careful, write to me, be good, and finally, "Good-bye, son." The car rounded the corner and dimmed from my sight.

Numbly, I ascended the five steps into the kitchen. I plopped onto a chair and stared at the crumbs on the kitchen floor. I warmed my hands around a cup of tea and began talking with One who was in the kitchen with me. "Father, thank You for Dan's new school. We need a house out there and Larry needs a job. I guess Dan is the most secure one of the bunch right now." I smiled when I thought of that.

It was only four days later when the phone awoke me. Rejection in Larry's voice traveled through the phone wires and reached into my very being. "Jane Lee, I'm bringing Daniel back home. He was endangering the severely handicapped children and cannot stay. The staff is so sorry...."

Was this my final exam of grace?

How many times did one family have to be wrung out?

Larry continued, "I called a Christian psychologist in another state, and he said Dan might have to be

Institutionalized." What an abominable word. How could a Christian psychologist suggest such a thing? I loathed him.

I hung up the phone and lay back on the pillow. Bitter disappointment and fear sickened me. As I stared at the white swirls in the plaster ceiling above my bed, I mused that there had to be help out there somewhere. Surely we could not live the rest of our lives being stalked in our own home. But I vowed, "*I WILL NEVER* institutionalize him - *NEVER!*"

And in my heart He seemed to say, "Oh?"

The "*I WILL NEVER...*" Chapter 18

(Or, "*I WILL NEVER* lose sight that Jesus is alive and reigns")

Larry burst into the kitchen. His countenance had been so downcast for so long, the change in expression was a welcome one. "Guess what?" he asked with the cat-who-caught-the-canary expression he usually reserved for Christmas. "O.K., I'll bite. What?" I responded. "Sit down. This will take a few minutes." I sat and fidgeted. "A social worker from the school that Daniel just left called. She was so burdened that they could not keep Dan that she has located another place that services aggressive children. It's a state facility, though…" I probed, "You mean it's a *government* institution?" He replied, "Yes."

On Becky's fifth birthday we flew to Illinois to check out the state mental health facility while Larry's parents cared for Daniel in Virginia.

It was a dreary, dismal, gray March day, giving no hints that spring would dawn the next day, when Larry and I drove in a borrowed van down the long driveway into the facility. I clung tightly to Larry's hand as he held open the heavy door for me to enter. The building had a distinctive, unpleasant aroma. The walls were drab, the atmosphere cold and institutional. We sat nervously in the cheerless waiting area.

I twisted my hands and inwardly prayed, "Father, surely this is not what you would want for our Dan. Surely this sterile place is not in your plan."

A social worker interrupted my thinking and invited us to her office. Her opening remark stung; "Of course, you realize institutionalization is the last resort."

Realize it? Did she really think we would be talking to her if we had not exhausted every other means? Did she think we just flew around the country at our whim? What kind of people was she used to dealing with?

She and two other staff interviewed us. She seemed wary that we would travel so far for help, willing to leave our home and job to get help for our son.

She refused to show us the unit where the children stayed, and I wondered if she were hiding something.

We boarded the ice-covered plane in Chicago for home, amazed at the Illinois spring weather as well as the Lord's grace in providing a new pastorate for Larry in Illinois.

Daniel's grandparents were devastated by their weekend with him. Each had a strong verbal reaction. My mother-in-law was perplexed as she said, "I don't see how you all keep your marriage going. Vernon and I have had no time to even speak to each other, and we have had to care for only one child." My father-in-law's glasses had been spindled, folded, and mutilated during the weekend, and his sad eyes reflected his grief behind the tilted glasses. He warned us, "You *must* get help for this child." He directed his next statement to me; "Jane, you know how much I love Larry. Well, if Larry were as sick as Dan is and were destroying everything in sight, I'd have him put in a hospital. You must get help. You must."

'Midst the dreary task of packing, we were startled with a delightful invitation to appear on our local Easter Seals Telethon. We unpacked some of our television debut clothes and were amazed at how well we all looked for a change. We cleaned up pretty nicely. We were jittery, however, not knowing if Dan would punch out the camera crew.

"Dan the Ham" shone in all of his glory. He waved to the camera, batted his eyelashes, showed his dimples, and answered the interviewer's questions loudly and as distinctly as he could. The slim television personality queried, "Dan, who helped you to walk again?" And Daniel happily replied, "Jesus did." The master of ceremonies tenaciously persisted, "And who else?" Dan dutifully responded, "Oh, Easter Seals."

Larry and I, reeling from the strain, drove home feeling as if we had been on television the entire twenty-four hours instead of three minutes.

When we appeared in the newspaper later in the week, I glanced around at all the empty boxes waiting to be packed, and decided I enjoyed being a short-termed celebrity more than packing.

One truck soon was filled with furniture and another truck was loaded with our Volkswagen Beetle, which in turn overflowed with bulging boxes. Two men from our new church drove the trucks to Illinois.

The difficult, tearful farewells to our precious church family began. I remembered how they had loved us in spite of the mistakes one makes in a first pastorate. I remembered how some had become Christians under Larry's ministry. I remembered the baptisms in the river and church picnics. I remembered how they had shared our suffering and how they, too, had felt the disappointment that Dan had progressed – yet not far enough.

As we bade good-bye to our parents, we could see in their eyes that they felt the same thing about us that we felt about Daniel - deep love but an inability to make everything all right.

The luscious green mountains passed and slowly smoothed into flat lands covered with rich, black soil.

The 700 mile trip was as horrendous as we had imagined it would be. Dan relentlessly attacked each one sitting next to him, so we played musical car seats for most of the trip. People in restaurants stared as our child gulped his food and then tried to grab his family's too. (On some occasions he snatched food from the tables of strangers).

It could not have been much harder in Conestoga wagons, and as the earlier pioneers heading west had done, we discovered some alternatives for survival. Alternative one: I sat in the back seat with David and Becky, and we strapped Daniel in the front seat, praying he would not grab the steering wheel. Alternative two: In restaurants, Larry fed Dan while the three of us quickly ate our meal, after which I would entertain Dan in the parking lot while Larry ate.

Seventeen hours later, we ate cold chicken off of packed cartons in the parsonage.

The next morning Easter dawned bright and glorious - and cold.

Out of the large picture window, I peered at the church steeple next door and then glanced down to the strangers who were beginning to arrive. I pressed my forehead against the glass and wistfully thought of our Virginia flock so far away.

Feeling misplaced, bone-weary, and homesick, I picked up my Bible and read the familiar Easter story. I could identify somewhat with the disciples when they too had felt "misplaced" when Jesus was in the tomb.

I read about Mary's weeping in the garden by the tomb. I was weeping, too.

I reached the climax of the story - "He is not here, He is risen!" (Matthew 28:6 KJV).

I knew this risen One loved me. He was in control of my life. "*I WILL NEVER* loose sight of the fact that Jesus is alive and reigns. NEVER."

And He, who had conquered death, seemed to ask in my heart, "Oh?"

The "*I WILL NEVER...*" Chapter 19

(Or, "*I WILL NEVER* believe God continually disappoints")

Scores of phone calls welcomed us to our new home. I attempted to be polite while ducking flying objects or literally barricading the refrigerator with my body to keep Daniel from eating all the contents therein. As I unpacked, Dan hurled pictures, lamps, and books at me. The soaring items marred the freshly painted parsonage walls. Not a good way to start a pastorate.

The days until the admission date at the mental health facility were marked off in my mind.

The night before his admission Dan disappeared from the driveway on his bicycle. Larry jumped into the car, and I searched on foot. Frightening thoughts flooded my heart. When Larry spotted his offspring vainly trying to get up off the ground, Daniel sheepishly peered over the handlebars and affirmed, "I know. I have the right to remain silent, and anything I say can be held against me."

The day of in-take finally came. The trunk was filled with carefully marked clothes, favorite books, a Bible, and beloved matchbox cars. The twenty-minute drive was a tense one. When we rounded the corner, the facility looked more forlorn than I had remembered.

We hesitated in the car, wondering whether or not to actually go through with this. Larry broke the silence and turned to me, "Jane, will you lead us in prayer?" Was he kidding? Pray with the boulder in my dry throat? Deciding it was easier to pray than to explain why I could not, I stammered, "Lord...," and that was that. The end. Amen. Tears overflowed my eyes, spilling onto my hands. Daniel began to pray, his eyes brimming with tears and his speech more slurred than usual. His drooling was worse. Larry closed in prayer.

We began the long walk into the dreary building, Larry and I each holding an eight-year-old hand.

The in-take was in a large room with about a dozen professionals sitting around a large oval table. As they studied the material on Daniel - how aggressive, unpredictable, and destructive he could be - he walked around the table and kissed each person. This sweet, affectionate, crippled child enraptured the mental health specialists. They seemed leery while questioning us, and I felt like a whining parent whose child had only repeatedly spilled milk over the last eighteen months.

Where is his aggression when we need it? Why doesn't he yank someone's hair? What's his problem?

After our interview we waited outside in the tall grass and bright sunshine while the staff discussed our perplexing case. I pulled nervously at the grass and wondered if the excruciating wait was akin to waiting for a jury's verdict.

90

The bearded psychologist summoned us. I felt uncomfortable as a female social worker smoked what, I wrongly thought, was a cigar. Colorful language was used freely, and I squirmed in my chair.

The psychologist carefully broke the dreaded news: Daniel did not fit in this place. The consensus of professional opinion ruled that Dan was not nearly ill enough to be at that facility. They felt he needed physical rehabilitation, and as he improved physically, he would improve emotionally.

I felt short of breath. My chest felt heavy. My heart felt shattered. We briefly thanked everyone and left. As we drove home in silence, I questioned God, "So what do you do with a person who is too sick for some hospitals and not sick enough for others?"

I entered the bright bedroom in the parsonage and unpacked the trunk once again and tried to prepare for more battles.

Dan mumbled about failing in two places now and feeling like the misfit he was. I held him close and whispered in his ear that his Daddy would never stop trying to get him help.

Larry stayed with Daniel while I went to the grocery store. I sat in the car and stared at the people passing by. "Father," I murmured, "Why would You bring us halfway across the country only to continually disappoint us?"

That evening after Becky was tucked in bed and sleep had finally come to Daniel after the long nightly bath battle, David joined me in the kitchen. Only the dim light above the oven shone and bounced off the new yellow gingham wallpaper. David seemed to sense my utter despair, and he said, almost apologetically, "Momma, if I had not saved Daniel's life by finding him after he fell, we wouldn't be going through all of this."

My first-born looked so tall in the dim light. His face reflected a crushed appearance, and I knew this was a rare moment together. "David," I began, silently praying for wisdom, "You feel guilty because you saved his life. Do you know that you would feel guilty if you had not saved his life? You're in a no-win situation, don't you think?"

David smiled the way one smiles when one is understood. He settled back into a chair and spilled the complicated emotions of a 12 year old. He talked about our moving, and new schools, and new friends, and the sovereignty of God. We had so little time to talk, and we reveled in our togetherness. The hour was getting late when he kissed me, and his relieved eyes sparkled in the dull light. "Good night, Mom," he said over his shoulder as his tall, lanky frame rounded the corner.

David had paid such a heavy price.

It was only a matter of days until we again packed Daniel's clothes and drove through the heavy traffic surrounded by tall buildings in Chicago. The run-down area made us hesitant to leave our car, much less our child. The ancient rehabilitation hospital's halls brimmed with elderly patients in various degrees of immobility. The place resembled a morgue and was undoubtedly the most depressing place I had ever seen. I did not want to leave a hyperactive, aggressive eight year old in something that was closely akin to a veteran's hospital. The admitting doctor stuttered, "We usually keep patients six weeks to two months."

After Daniel was admitted to his stark white room, he commented to the nurse, "Now this is my kind of place." He was more desperate to fit in than we had dreamed.

On our first visit we found Dan in restraints because he had gotten up early and had been roaming the halls. On our next visit the security guard stared at us as we signed in.

The hospital administrator abruptly stopped us in the hall. His face was tense and tired looking, with deep lines showing in his forehead. "Your son has caused quite a bit of excitement here today," he began. I was not sure I wanted him to go on, but he continued, "Your son walked out of the hospital, proceeded down the street, and entered a restaurant...or bar... and asked a stranger to buy him some food. When we realized he was gone, we turned this hospital upside-down to find him. Daniel finally showed up outside. I have ordered tighter security for the entire hospital." The administrator shook his head as he left us.

The thought of Dan walking down the street in that area unnerved me, but he simply explained, "Mom, all I did was ride the elevator down, walk out the door, and when I got to this eatin' place, I asked a man sitting on a tall stool to buy me some cereal. And he bought me some food. Then I thanked him and came back to the hospital."

My legs turned to mush, hearing this.

The six weeks to two months stay was shortened to four days. Dan had hurt an elderly, immobile man and was a constant threat to other patients.

Dejectedly, we drove home through the busy streets. I set down the small suitcase in our living room, and my son quickly twisted my necklace around my neck, strangling me. Back to battle. Back to survival. I lay wearily in bed that night. Sleep would not come to grant relief.

"God, are you toying with our emotions? Are you watching any of this? Where are you? *I WILL NEVER* believe you could get glory through our family."

And in my heart He seemed to say, "Oh?"

The "*I WILL NEVER...*" Chapter 20

(Or, "*I WILL NEVER* despair...")

In less than a week we sat in the small waiting area of the familiar state mental health facility. Seated across from us, a young fearful girl clutched a brown paper bag. I looked at her hollow eyes and wondered where her parents were.

The social worker startled me when she suddenly appeared to show us the hitherto unseen unit. As I rose slowly to follow her down the hall, I wondered what new world lay behind the closed doors.

Although the three large rooms with numerous beds were not homey, they were clean. The social worker glared at me and warned, "I sure hope that trunk isn't full of clothes because there's no room for them." I had expected a compliment for having Daniel so well prepared. I wanted to explain that this trunk had been packed and unpacked many times recently, but I simply chuckled a nervous laugh with no comment.

As Larry signed more papers in a nearby office, I overheard his pleading, "You are sure these papers don't make him a ward of the state? He still is my boy, isn't he? There's no fine print here that makes him yours and not mine, is there?"

We kissed Daniel, assured him we would pray for him, and quickly exited the unit. The social worker proudly proclaimed, "We're damn good, and we'll have him shaped up in six weeks." Larry and I walked back down the long walk, wondering what magic these professionals could wield to accomplish in six weeks what we had not been able to accomplish in eighteen months.

Larry treated the whole family at a local steak house that evening. We each felt euphoric when we realized we could eat leisurely with no threat of someone eating our food. "Is the baked potato really this succulent or have we just not tasted our food in a year and a half?" I asked Larry. He was too busy stuffing his mouth to answer. In fact, no one waxed conversational as little hands and big hands slowly put food into little mouths and big mouths and chewed each bite in slow motion, eyes at half-mast. I was musing if other patrons were observing us, wondering if we had just come in from a refugee camp. At the end of the meal David skillfully balanced the saltshaker on several grains of salt. We clapped. We acted like a normal family. Felt good, too.

We drove into the parsonage driveway as the sun was sinking over the church steeple. "Okay, kids, it's time for baths and bed. School starts in the morning. Let's hustle, you two." Two? Setting my purse on the kitchen table, I thought about Daniel settling in at a strange place for the night. I took comfort when I realized it was only for six weeks. "*I WILL NEVER* let him stay longer."

And He, who knows the future, seemed to say in my heart, "Oh?"

The "*I WILL NEVER...*" Chapter 21

(Or, "*I WILL NEVER* forget this Memorial Day")

The three weeks of separation slowly passed until we were allowed to visit our son. Daniel heard our voices, and when the big doors were unlocked, he leaped into the air, ascending on our necks, hugging all of us at once.

We gaily walked into the brilliant warm day, and as we sat in the tall grass, I fed him applesauce. We were being observed through the large windows by either staff or patients, but it mattered not a bit. We played on the gym equipment with other emotionally disturbed children until it was time for us to leave. Dan sobbed uncontrollably and clung to our clothing. None of us ever got used to that.

Memorial Day was unseasonably warm, and we packed chicken for a picnic with Daniel. It would be good to see him again. As the heavy doors were unlocked, the strong odor of urine carried by warm air pierced our noses. A patient had wet the bed the night before, and the stench had been growing all day on the unchanged linen.

We basked in the fresh air as we spread our blanket down and meted out the chicken.

"Son, why are you so dirty and are wearing only shorts?" I asked. Daniel quickly replied, "Oh, Mom, it's a holiday, and I haven't had time to do my laundry yet." Larry secured permission to bathe him, and I combed his drawers for clean clothes. Every drawer was empty. In utter desperation, David took off underwear, a shirt, and socks and gave them to his brother. As David stood in his cut-off shorts, he warned, "Folks, this is all I'm donating."

Again, we left with heavy hearts hearing Dan's screams echoing down the empty halls. "Please don't leave me here...please..." We literally ran to the car to escape the cries, and five-year-old Becky's short legs struggled to keep up with us. When Larry opened the car door for me, I said, "Larry, *I WILL NEVER* get used to this."

And I never did.

The following weeks we were being trained by staff to become better parents - "standard procedure" we were told. I thought this implied we were part of Dan's problem and not part of the solution. One of our teachers told us she got so angry with her child that she once beat him with her fists. I could not believe we had to sit weekly under her lessons in parenting.

It was extremely difficult to sift through the deluge of material we were supposed to incorporate in our parenting. Some of it we could agree with; some we definitely did not. We were kept off-kilter.

We struggled. It was spiritual warfare, and we were keenly involved in the battle. We wanted to learn, but we prayed constantly for wisdom to discern what was truth and what was error.

"Father, *I WILL NEVER* understand your way. We have no choice but to come to these parenting sessions. *I WILL NEVER* understand why You are allowing this in our lives."

And He, who is Wisdom, seemed to say in my heart, "Oh?"

The "*I WILL NEVER...*" Chapter 22

(Or, "*I WILL NEVER* forget this human sandwich")

Six weeks of hope had long since passed. The psychologist remorsefully admitted, "He's a sicker boy than we thought. In fact, he's a better patient than we are therapists."

The rigors of a new pastorate, unpleasant visits with Dan on the unit, the weekly parental training session -— plus homework to sift through, as well as the weekly meetings with the psychologist and social workers were crushing. The combination of all these combined with the loneliness of a move so far from home took its emotional toll on me.

I was overwhelmed with guilt. I felt our son's removal from our home was a personal assault on the job -— being a mother -— which I valued more than any on earth. I felt demoted. Humiliated. Replaced. The tantalizing heaviness of inadequacy bled into other areas of my life conjuring doubts - *I'm probably not a good pastor's wife, or mother to my other two children, or wife to Larry.*

I kept all of these feelings pushed way down in my soul while we were at the many meetings at the facility. Larry was our "appointed" spokesman, and that saved me from any emotional scenes. My seething anger erupted the minute we got in the car for home. "Larry, you didn't say that right..." or "Larry, you should've said..." or "Larry, as head of our home, why do you let us keep suffering?"

Those were days of conflict about new philosophies being hurled at us as well as days of conflict about whether we were doing the right things.

The nagging conflicts greeted me each morning and put me to sleep each night.

It was a typically windy midwestern day when our family drove Dan from his unit to a grassy knoll on the grounds of

Scarce tender moment David, Larry, Becky and Daniel

the mental health facility. Larry set up his sketch board and paints, David steadied them against the strong winds, and Becky, Dan, and I sat on the blanket. After our open-air Sunday school together, Dan asked if we all could just snuggle. All five of us snuggled as closely as we dared on our ragged blanket on these psychiatric grounds. We made a human sandwich with Mom and Dad being the "bread" enveloping three slices of wiggling, giggling "ham."

Sitting up and leaning on one hand for balance, Larry asked his replica, "Daniel, do you understand why Mom and Dad had to get help for you here? Do you understand how much we love you? Do you understand how much God loves you and wants His best for you?"

Leaning back on his left arm, his legs partially crossed, Daniel did not talk. He began singing in his halting speech,

> *I am not skilled to understand*
> *What God hath willed, what*
> *God hath planned,*
> *I only know at His right hand*
> *Stands One who is my Savior.*

We took him into our arms, and our tears spilled down his neck. Silently, I thanked God for this precious moment and Daniel's spiritual insight.

Moments later, when Dan returned to the unit, he again began hysterically begging us not to leave him. The heavy doors again locked behind us, separating this "bone of our bone and flesh of our flesh" from us.

"Although it hurts to have a tender heart, Lord, *I WILL NEVER* become hardened."

And He, who is meek and lowly of heart, seemed to ask in mine, "Oh?"

The "*I WILL NEVER...*" Chapter 23

(Or, "*I WILL NEVER* get through this")

Staff unlocked the door at 6:30 a.m. and abruptly asked, "What are *you* doing here?" The staff was about as glad to see us, as we were to see them. Seated in an enclosed glass area on the unit, we were there to observe Dan's morning routine as had been requested by the psychologist.

Although our son was overcome with joy to see us, he was instructed to ignore us and go about his "routine." It was a super-human expectation, but he cooperated unusually well. He brushed his teeth with extra diligence and proudly came to our area to show them to me. Because that was considered an infraction of the rules, he was whisked off to a locked "cell" for a time-out. His mournful yells penetrated the whole area and seeped behind our glass enclosure.

Since I had complimented Dan on his good job of teeth brushing, I felt that I should have been timed-out also as an accessory to the crime. I could not fathom that showing his teeth to his mother whom he saw once a week merited such drastic punishment.

As screams escalated during the twenty minutes, hatred seethed in my heart toward the staff as they merrily went about their duties, seemingly unmoved by the haunting sounds. "Humph," I whispered to Larry, "that psychologist promised us at in-take that they would not love Dan, but they would only care for him. They sure make good on their promises." I did not translate their coolness as professionalism but as hardness. My perception was clouded with heavy emotion, and the scene sickened me.

After the time-out we hesitantly observed Daniel at breakfast. Other emotionally disturbed children occupied the long tables in the small cafeteria. I made every effort to be polite and appear cheery, but when someone offered me coffee, I knew I would throw up if I drank any. Even Larry – stalwart Larry – looked a bit green around the gills.

I glanced around the room, trying to divert my attention from our son's attempts to open a sealed milk carton with one hand. I sat on my own hands, resisting the temptation to help him. The battle with the carton was a lengthy one, and just as the carton yielded to his persistence, the milk spilled onto the floor. Before I could speak, the staff snapped, "OK, Dan, go get a mop and clean this up." My first reaction was to grab her by the collar and shout, "Have you ever tried to open a milk carton with one hand?" Daniel was busily mopping before I could compose myself long enough to speak, and then words came only to encourage my son.

The children soon shoved, shouted obscenities, and scowled at each other as they lined up for the school, which was just across the grassy field located on the grounds of the mental health facility. I had never heard children swear to such an extreme and was visibly shaken. Pulling my face down to his, Dan leaned against the wall and whispered, "Momma, I don't talk like that because my life verse says 'Daniel purposed in his heart that he would not defile himself....'" (Daniel 1:8 KJV)

I stood back against the wall and smiled. Joy burst within my soul. In my heart I chanted, "Praise the Lord." In my adulation, I almost missed the staff talking softly to Larry. "Oh, yes, Daniel does too swear. We don't encourage it, but we do allow it."

It was 8:30 a.m. – so early for so much gloom. A whole day stretched before me to hear the moans reverberating in my memory.

It was only a matter of days until we were invited to share our observations of Dan's morning routine. The sun glistened through the window while Larry shared our feelings. Typically, I sat silent. The staff listened intently to Larry's description of our hurts and wounded spirits. Her response was unexpected. "I am so sorry. It never dawned on me that you and Dan would want to be close. You see I've never worked with a normal family before. The families I have worked with do not want to be close."

"*I WILL NEVER* get through this. *Never.*"

And He, who is Strength, seemed to say in my heart, "Oh?"

The "*I WILL NEVER...*" Chapter 24

(Or, "*I WILL NEVER* get angry")

So, how do you Christians handle anger?" queried the therapist. I glanced over at Larry. He shifted his eyes as he thought of this unusual question. I jumped in where angels fear to tread; "Oh, we just don't get real angry." That sounded pious enough, though untrue. The therapist smiled knowingly, and I added, "Well, I mean, sometimes we get kind of mad, but we just hold it in. We don't explode or anything." It was one of those statements that you wish you could retract the minute it leaves your mouth. I settled back in the uncomfortable chair, crossed my arms, and smiled an embarrassed smile, knowing I had dug a deep hole.

Trying to worm my way out of the conversation, I continued, "Well, I mean, I know Christians with repressed anger get ulcers just like non-Christians with repressed anger. But, uh, we..." My eyes shot over to Larry for assistance, but he remained silent and seemed anxious to see how I would get out of the hole I just dug. I do believe he was almost smiling.

What I meant to say is, "We just kind of ignore anger." Larry's eyes rolled in disbelief, knowing that when I am angry, no one in our family can readily ignore it.

There was little resolved in that office that day, and as we drove home, we talked about my inability to respond about Christians and anger. Larry purposed to do a study in the Bible on anger and correct responses to it.

There was a light frost on the ground as I traveled to a weekend conference in Indiana where Dr. James Dobson, Christian psychologist and conference speaker, was leading a workshop. As he spoke, my soul lapped up the gentle words as cool refreshing water. Because I had been saturated for months with psychology from a different perspective, the contrast was vivid. After I returned home, I excitedly related to my husband some of the things I had learned. And without my knowledge, Larry placed a phone call to Dr. Dobson in California to receive more insights on Christians and anger.

It was suppertime. Things were boiling on the stove, meat was sizzling in the broiler, and visiting children were everywhere in our house in varied stages of playful loud voices. The ringing telephone irritated me as I grabbed it and nestled it against my shoulder, leaving hands free to cook.

"Hello, Mrs. Bateman," greeted a warm voice. "This is Dr. James Dobson's secretary. Dr. Dobson is returning your husband's call."

My eyes widened. The louder decibels and the crescendo of children's voices throughout the house prevailed, despite my hands signaling them to be quiet. After all, a child psychologist on the line may overhear and analyze us all. I purred into the phone something about David going to get his Dad next door at the church office and then conveniently rested the phone on the kitchen table while I spoke in melodious sugary tones to startled children, hoping to impress the good doctor. Larry flew in the door and breathlessly greeted Doctor Dobson. Nervously, I stirred food that did not need stirring, straining my ears to overhear all this wisdom oozing about on our bedroom phone.

Dr. Dobson expressed enormous compassion. It felt good. He gave Biblical insights into anger as well. He cautioned, "Of course, I am very far away and have not met Daniel, but I suspect he is more grief-stricken over his loss than he is angry." It was several weeks later that Dr. Dobson sent us a recording of one of his conference talks and this note of encouragement:

> *Dear Mrs. Bateman,*
>
> *God loves you and your family, and He will not abandon you now! I've been praying for you and know that He feels for you "as a father pities his child." Daniel will make it!*
>
> *Keep your faith in spite of the unbelieving professionals. Perhaps you will win them too!*
>
> *God bless you,*
>
> *Jim Dobson*

We met with the professionals at the mental health facility with more confidence. We, too, had felt all along that our son was not as full of rage as he was overwhelmed with grief. When we carefully detailed our feelings to the therapist, he responded, "We do not know how to treat grief.

But we do know how to treat anger. We'll call it anger – not grief."

The cool smell of winter pierced our noses as we walked to the car in the parking lot. "I know One who is acquainted with grief...a Man of sorrows," I thought to myself. Those attributes comforted me. "Isn't it marvelous to know that Dan belongs to One who understands every emotion?" I asked Larry. He squeezed my hand in agreement.

Along the highway the ugly smokestacks belched their gray guts, and I realized how different this scenery was from our smooth green mountains in our quiet Virginia valley. "You know, Larry, we have come so far to get help, and it's been six months – not six weeks – of hospitalization, and they still don't know how to treat him. They are not even sure what to label his problem."

Later that evening, I sat in the blue chair in our large living room in the church parsonage. I leaned my head back and thought about anger and grief and a hundred other emotions.

"*I WILL NEVER* let my complicated emotions get the best of me."

And He, who understands all the garbled emotions of mothers and daddies and children, seemed to ask in my heart, "Oh?"

The "*I WILL NEVER...*" Chapter 25

(Or, "*I WILL NEVER* accept blame")

My back arched, and my maternal claws protruded when a consulting psychologist entered Dan's perplexing case and suggested, "Maybe he had problems before he fell, and they are just surfacing now."

I surprised everyone, including myself, when this "woman's scorn" was unleashed. Although we did not meet with the consultant, I attacked the bearer of his opinion.

"Look, Dan's problems have nothing to do with how he was raised. You're not throwing that guilt trip at my feet. He was a totally normal little boy who has sustained massive brain damage. Just because you can't cure him, your professional pride is hurt, and you want to pretend the problems were there all along. Well, you are wrong!" I shrieked.

My voice cracked. My hands shook. I crossed my trembling legs, trying to steady them. My face was flushed. And I was mortified at my outburst.

The room stayed hushed for a long time. I felt awkward. Larry, in a calm manner, explained, "We are all victims of his fall. But Daniel was a happy, active, average seven year old when he fell."

I slid down in my chair a bit.

Our arguments sounded hollow. We were saying things parents are supposed to say.

Seated in the small office, the social worker asked, "So, why was Daniel in the top bunk anyway?" I thought I sensed cynicism in her voice. What I heard was, "What were you thinking, woman, to have allowed him to be on the top bunk?"

I rapidly justified our sleeping arrangements. "The boys always rotated from top bunk to bottom bunk on the days I changed linen. We had a rail up. A ladder. We had carpeting on the floor. I never dreamed..." My voice trailed off.

I leaned back in the small chair and wondered if I had been convincing in my closing defensive arguments. "Why do I feel as if I am on trial?" I wondered.

It was not long after that bitter encounter that Daniel came home for a short visit. Having been convinced by staff that perhaps we were partially responsible for Dan's injury, we both asked him to forgive us for buying bunk beds. He quickly offered his forgiveness with a hug to seal it.

Sidling up to me in the kitchen, our son sweetly remarked, "Momma, I can just imagine how it'd be to live here with you 'cause this home is such a 'happiness place." It was at such rare tender moments that the separations became almost intolerable.

Armed with chocolate chip cookies and his little suitcase, Daniel climbed into the front seat of the car to leave our "happiness place" for the mental health facility. Tears streamed down his face as he waved good-bye to his brother and sister.

"Father," I prayed silently as I turned out of our driveway, "Let this dear boy move back home. *I WILL NEVER* last through another six months of painful separation."

And He, whose Home is the ultimate "Happiness Place," seemed to ask in my heart, "Oh?"

The "*I WILL NEVER...*" Chapter 26

(Or, "*I WILL NEVER* forget this dry stuffing and plastic bulbs")

The succulent aroma of the turkey greeted our noses as we walked through the parsonage door from the Thanksgiving service at the church. All of Daniel's favorite foods awaited his arrival for the day. Adding some broth to the dry dressing, I smiled, "There's so little I can do for my boy, I especially love cooking for him," I said to myself as I licked the spoon.

David, Becky and I ran to the door to greet Larry and Dan. I helped Daniel take off his brown and white coat.

"Dan, just wait till you see what I fixed..." I happily announced, anxious to recite my lengthy, luscious menu. Daniel nonchalantly interrupted me as he walked toward the television, "I've already eaten. The staff gave us an early lunch."

The afternoon deteriorated after that. Daniel cried all afternoon and wildly ran out of the door and down the street twice. I recorded in my diary, "As I ran down the block after Dan, all the homes looked full of relatives. I secretly envied everyone who has family close by with healthy children."

I wistfully remembered two years earlier on Thanksgiving when I had expected God to heal Daniel. It had only been two years? Not 200?

There was not even a hint of healing. In fact, things were worsening. The aggressions were more frequent and more severe. Dan had numerous black eyes, cuts, scratches, and huge knots on his head. Some came from other patients, and some were results of self-abuse.

The December snows buried everything, and the warm office at the mental health facility thawed our frozen hands as we met with the psychologist. He reported unemotionally, "Daniel is not progressing. There are two things we have not tried: medication and no home visits for ninety days."

Quickly up in arms, Larry argued, "WE WILL NEVER stand for discontinuing home visits. We need input in his life. The child desperately needs his family. He needs the warmth of a home one day a week, at least."

The therapist was unconvinced. Numb in spirit, we walked slowly to the car. While scraping the car windows, Larry's face mirrored his brokenness. Crushed and dull of heart, we departed for home.

My diary reads, "How much more will the Lord allow us to go through? It almost seems as if He doesn't care, though I know He does."

I swiveled about in the kitchen chair. Resting on the wall above the beige Priscilla curtains, a plaque bore the meaning of my name. I read it out loud: "Jane – God's gracious gift." The Bible verse below it poured oil over my aching heart: "The Lord will give grace and glory. No good thing will He withhold from them that walk uprightly" (Psalm 84:11 KJV).

I fiddled with the plastic flower arrangement on the table and wondered about grace and glory and His not withholding things from His children.

The phone startled me as an unwelcome intruder. The therapist spoke rapidly as he told me they had called in another consultant. He suggested that since Dan seemed to be more comfortable being a patient, he had a good chance of being institutionalized for life if his home visits were taken away. There was a pause while I caught my breath. The psychologist continued, "The consultant asked an interesting question: If the hospitalization here is not working, why do you want to increase it? I suggest you *increase* his time at home." I blubbered with joy into the phone.

I walked into the dining room, my heart as light as the angel hair surrounding the Christmas angel on the table.

I waltzed around the table and sang, "I knew we were therapeutic." I danced back into the kitchen to check on the pies I was making for all our church families. I set the warm pies on the counter to cool and remembered, "No good thing will He withhold from them..."

After supper we gathered around the phone to call Daniel. Staff answered robot-style, "He is sleeping. He has a cold. He cannot talk." I wanted to reply, "Merry Christmas to you, too." But I refused to let any cold staff chill this warm feeling in my heart.

Several hours later we called again. Dan finally came to the phone, crying and moaning into the receiver. His words were unintelligible. Staff retrieved the phone and again the robotic report was, "He just woke up. He is tired."

Something was wrong.

The next morning, on Christmas Eve, David and Becky peered out of the frosty picture window. Tall David rearranged Christmas balls on the tree. Becky counted the minutes until she could open her gifts – something she was promised she could do as soon as Dan came home.

A few plastic ornaments lay next to the tree so that Daniel would be able to decorate some.

The car motor hummed in the driveway, and I ran to peek out of the window, almost stepping on the manger scene.

"Here he comes," shouted Becky. It always amazed me that someone so tiny could make such loud announcements.

The red velvet bow and clanging bell dropped snow on the floor as David flung open the door for his Dad and brother.

Larry's face looked ashen. Lifeless. Hurt.

He set the small blue suitcase inside and helped his stumbling son up the parsonage steps. Eyes at half-mast, Dan stumbled into the living room and collapsed on the sofa.

Submerged in sorrow, Larry quietly explained that Daniel had developed severe asthma and diarrhea as a reaction to a new drug. He was given large doses of Mellaril without our consent or knowledge and was in a stupor. Larry had found Dan on the unit too sedated to go to the bathroom, and he had to clean up the diarrhea before he could bring his son home.

Dan lay on the couch. Other than the heaving of his chest, he lay motionless. He looked as if he had expired.

I whispered to Larry that I refused to believe our son would not wake up for new toys. We placed Dan under the tree, and he keeled over into the packages.

Back to the sofa with the body.

David and Becky stared in disbelief at their brother, and our living room took on the atmosphere of a Christmas wake. I sat on the floor by the sofa and held Dan's hand. The plastic red bulbs lying by the tree were blurred through my tears. My husband sank into a chair, looking as if he had been flogged.

David and Becky worked around their brother's limp body and tore open their gifts. We pretended to have fun. I sarcastically remarked to my husband, "Who cares there is a corpse-like nine year old on the sofa? Who cares there are his unopened gifts waiting under the tree? Who cares the staff did not hint to us that he is over sedated? I hope the doctor who prescribed this medication is having a rotten day. I mean rotten." My Christmas spirit was definitely on the decline.

Twenty-five hours later, Daniel began to awaken. He overheard an advertisement on television about "The Bear Who Slept Through Christmas," and he mumbled in a soft whisper, "Momma, I guess I'm that bear."

Eventually, he opened presents, but he did not have the strength to play with them. We returned Daniel to the facility on Christmas night with stern warnings to staff that there be no excessive drugs given. We asked for more information on Mellaril and found it was a "drug effective in reducing excitement, hyper mobility, abnormal initiative... through its inhibitory effect on psychomotor functions." I asked, "In other words, too much of the stuff and it can conveniently 'zombie-ize' a person on holidays when people don't want to be bothered with him?" No one answered.

When we reached home, David asked Larry and me to open our gifts. Our lips said "thank you," but our hearts were torn asunder as we opened the presents.

I lay in bed. Nauseous. Cold.

I remembered the Christmas two years earlier when Daniel had been comatose. We had not come far.

"Father," I prayed, "Was separation from your Son this excruciating?"

I sang Happy Birthday to Him quietly, so as not to wake my husband who was sleeping next to me.

"*I WILL NEVER* forget that I have a Savior who understands separation."

And He, who knew all about anguish and pain, seemed to ask in my heart, "Oh?"

The "*I WILL NEVER...*" Chapter 27

(Or, "*I WILL NEVER* allow our home to become a battleground")

Our jaws set, our eyes fiery, our arguments rehearsed, we drove to the mental health hospital as if going into battle. We were to spar in person with the consulting psychiatrist who had earlier mentioned Dan might have had emotional problems before his fall. He also had prescribed the heavy doses of medication at Christmas.

I arranged my armor, so to speak, and entered the office. *You don't wanna mess with this Momma, Doc.*

The psychiatrist did not appear as I had pictured him. He had no forked tongue. He did not slither into the office and coil up on a chair ready to strike. He pleasantly greeted us and affirmed, "Rev. and Mrs. Bateman, I can see you love your son very much. You both have done an excellent job with him." Larry mumbled a surprised "thank you" while I let my armor slip to the floor unnoticed.

No one had commended us in so long that we both "purred" and "begged" for more.

The meeting was a short one, and Larry held my arm as we walked down the corridors of the facility. Larry asked in disbelief, "Jane, did he really say we had done a good job? Did you hear what I think I heard?"

We were still basking in the compliments several days later when Dan came home for a visit. It was a cold, snowy Saturday when each of us was seated in our living room watching recordings of our last vacation together in Myrtle Beach, South Carolina. The core of happy memories was encrusted in a shell of sadness. Dan, still sedated and groggy, slumped in his chair while David attempted to cheer everyone. "Look, Dan, look how your finger is sticking up out of the water like a periscope." Daniel bolted out of the room, falling in the hall. He beat his paralyzed right hand with his left fist, knowing that finger could no longer be extended.

In several weeks a brave dentist – perhaps with kamikaze training – agreed to cap Dan's front tooth, which had been chipped "while falling," said staff; "while being hit in the mouth," said Daniel. In less than a day Daniel pulled off the cap in a fit of anger, and in less than a week another patient socked him in the jaw, and he lost another tooth completely.

A professional later wrote in his evaluation, "Dan is more aggressive overall, but he is relating better to peers." I found this hard to comprehend since he had both eyeteeth knocked out in two weeks.

Larry took our son to a major children's hospital in Chicago for an outpatient check-up. The physician indicated the brain damage was permanent and we should not expect much improvement in behavior nor coordination. And because of such a limited attention span, the doctor thought

Dan might have to have a one on one instruction in a residential school for the rest of his life. She then added, "He has made remarkable progress, and you and your wife have done a good job." Another compliment? Maybe there was a pattern forming.

Daniel's teacher was hospitalized for a week after he kicked her. The next home visit was no better, with his biting and kicking me and trying to tear David apart. After each bout with David, Becky rushed into her room to retrieve her stale Halloween candy, hoping to soothe David's heart. After the long afternoon battles and relentless warfare, I decided in desperation to let the children work it out among themselves as they do in normal families. After Daniel hurled a glass and dish at David's head, I closed my eyes and instructed, "Okay, David, you handle him." I peeked long enough to see David literally pick up his brother and toss him in slow motion onto the cushioned sofa. It was a magnificent display of controlled anger.

Peace reigned for a moment.

Becky called her daddy home from the church office because we were fading fast and needed fresh troops.

After Daniel had grabbed and tried to throw the television, he was taken to bed. He leaned against his dresser and sobbed, "Please let me sleep in David's room like I did before I was hurt. I want the old Daniel back." Larry gently tucked him in his own bed, and he remorsefully wept, "I just wish there was somebody on this earth who could understand what it's like."

I wearily walked into the kitchen and faced the dishes waiting for me in the sink. Some had been thrown at me earlier that evening. My leg was oozing blood where Dan had bitten me. I leaned against the sink and thought, "I love

Daniel with every part of my being, but *I WILL NEVER* allow our home to become a battleground. *NEVER.*"

And He, in whose Home is perfect harmony, seemed to ask in my heart, "Oh?"

The "*I WILL NEVER...*" Chapter 28

(Or, "*I WILL NEVER* do what that church member just did")

I was embarrassed. It was humiliating for me to go to our midweek prayer meeting at church every Wednesday with the same prayer request. The familiar scene had occurred each week for months. Larry asked for prayer requests, and little Becky Bateman's five-year-old hand shot up excitedly. "Pray for Daniel," she drawled. And so the people prayed. And Dan's behavior worsened.

I sugarcoated my pride and bitterness and sweetly purred in the parsonage, "Becky, honey, these people know Dan is very sick. I'm sure they'll pray for him without your asking each week. We need to give others a chance to talk."

She never asked for prayer again.

I was pricked by the verse, "But whosoever shall offend one of these little ones which believe in Me, it were better for him that a millstone were hanged about his neck...." (Matthew 18:6 KJV).

Several months later, we were again in prayer meeting. I was weary in soul and body. Carrying a millstone is no light matter. The week had been devastating, with Daniel's having been in restraints almost four hours, his having broken his speech therapist's glasses, and his having kicked his school teacher yet again.

Larry had no spring in his step as he walked toward the podium in the fellowship hall of our church. His dull eyes were expressionless. He spoke in uncharacteristically low tones. "Please pray for our Daniel. Things are worsening," he reported in halting words.

Someone quickly interrupted, "Well, I still say, what he needs is less talking and a good old-fashioned spanking. I think he's sick of talk, and the pressure you put on him is too much." Members of the congregation squirmed.

Silence.

Becky glanced up at me for my reaction.

David stared at his dad for his reaction.

I shuffled my Bible in my lap and pretended to flip through it. I was cut to the quick, and I wanted to slap the woman.

Ignoring the lady's admonition, Larry proceeded with his short sermon, and I admired him for his unwavering persistence.

I quickly left after the meeting, not tarrying to talk. I popped some popcorn and sat at the kitchen table in the dark eating it and thought about the church member's advice. How does a parent discipline a child who has *no* impulse control at times and *little* impulse control at others? I remembered the psychologist warning us, "We realize we have you 'over a barrel'. But if you go against our treatment plan and spank him, we'll just give your kid back to you."

I remembered our other children's complaints that it was not fair that their brother could demolish our home and only get put in time-out. I stirred the un-popped kernels in the bottom of the bowl and prayed, "Father, we desperately need your wisdom. Thank you that your Word has promised that if we lack wisdom, all we need to do is ask for it. I'm asking. Begging. Pleading!"

Confused and conflicted, we continued to use time-out during Dan's home visits, hoping to be consistent with the hospital's treatment plan.

Larry had put locks on our mudroom door so we could use it for a time-out room (A mudroom is a necessary entrance room in the Midwest designed for boots and coats. It usually, however, stores mittens, hats, scarves, book bags, lunch boxes, brief cases, groceries, garbage, pets, soda bottles, brooms, mops, and mail.) Our mudroom was stripped bare.

One evening during supper, Dan hurled most of the food at us, and Larry and I hurried to harness the swinging arms, kicking legs, and sharp teeth into the mudroom. I quickly locked the door and breathed a sigh of relief. Sitting back down to the table, I innocently asked, "Where's Daddy?" The pounding on the door alerted me that in my haste to lock the door, I had also locked Larry in time-out with Daniel.

After Larry was "released," I meekly tried to apologize, but I began laughing. Larry interpreted my apology as not being sincere since it was accompanied by hysterical laughter. A stinging lecture followed on the impropriety of laughing at the wrong time, which made David, Becky, and me snicker all the more.

After we retrieved our food, which was in various places throughout the kitchen, we sat and tried to eat. Dan's pounding and screaming permeated the heavy silence.

Picking at my food, I prayed, "I asked you for wisdom. *I WILL NEVER* figure out why you don't seem to give it."

And I pictured Him smiling when He seemed to ask, "Oh?"

The "*I WILL NEVER...*" Chapter 29

(Or, "*I WILL NEVER* understand saintly anonymous script")

"Job's comforters" began springing up here and there. Most remained anonymous in unsigned letters "lovingly advising" us. Some suggested, as did one of Job's friends, "My advice to you is this: Go to God and confess your sins..." Others expressed concern about demons. Others inquired how we could have "put Daniel away." Others advised we "speak in tongues and claim healing already provided at the cross."

Larry and I wrestled with each letter, taking none lightly.

First, we agonized over the advice to "confess your sins." I met Larry in his study at the church and we wrestled with the problem of sin in our lives. We re-examined our hearts together lest there be any unconfessed sin and we felt confident the sin question was taken care of. We read John chapter 9 where some other parents had been accused of sin because their son was born blind. We were comforted in the fact that Jesus had answered that the man's blindness was not due to sin.

Second, we studied about demons. We reached the awesome conclusion that demons cannot filtrate where the blood of Jesus has been applied. Daniel was a believer. We were convinced the demons had to pass over.

Third, we mournfully re-evaluated why Dan was not in our home. This was, by far, the most difficult issue. We could only use common sense that we had a responsibility to protect our children and ourselves against one so violent and dangerous. Gnawing at us was the unrelenting question – were we sacrificing Daniel's life for the welfare of David and Becky? We knew, before God, we did not hospitalize Dan for convenience sake but because he needed help and we needed protection – in that order.

And fourth, as for the charismatic emphasis, we had prayed, sought with tears of grief, fasted, and anointed our son with oil, and the Lord had not granted healing.

We dared not share these letters from the "brethren" with the professionals working with us because we felt they would be a poor testimony to any non-Christians working with our family.

Sharing these letters only with each other and taking frequent spiritual inventory because of the suggestions contained in them, we fluctuated between turmoil and tranquility.

After receiving one unusually stern letter, I knelt beside my bed, rested my head on the bedspread, and prayed, "Father, give me wisdom in my dealings with others, especially those who are hurting. Help me not to judge when I have so little knowledge of their circumstances. *I WILL NEVER* presume that I could take someone else's situation and glibly give unsolicited advice."

The One who is not limited in His knowledge of our lives seemed to ask in my heart, "Oh?"

The "*I WILL NEVER...*" Chapter 30

(Or, "*I WILL NEVER* neglect our other children")

"I really hate going out there to see Dan," erupted David. He hated the stench and seeing other pitiful children. There was an autistic child, when not heavily sedated, who sat in the corner for hours at a time, knotting everyone's shoelaces together. A schizophrenic boy was into smelling armpits when not clawing faces. Other little children, there through no fault of their own, called us "Mom and Dad" and begged to go home with us. I was critical of David's balking at visiting until in an honest moment I realized I did not like going to the hospital either. I was just not as vocal about it as my son.

When Daniel came home for visits, David spent every Friday night and all day Saturday being part of our "staff." We rotated our duties around a demanding boy, and he demanded the most from David, whom he idolized.

Daniel wanted to play as they had played before he was hurt and before the clock had stopped. David felt foolish as a budding teenager playing with childish toys. Although David was always assaulted in return for his perseverance in play, he seldom complained.

I scarcely had time to notice David's patience. It never occurred to me that siblings have less commitment than do parents, and my expectations of our oldest son were unrealistically high. It was much later that I realized the responsibility David felt to protect me when his daddy was at church studying. More than once, he tried to wrestle Dan off of me while Becky breathlessly stood by the phone with one finger on the dial trying in vain to remember her daddy's office number. (After so long we wised up and wrote the number down for her. Those days were before speed dialing, much less cell phones.)

After a harrowing weekend our lanky junior high boy started out to school. He turned in the doorway and looking over his shoulder, he remarked wistfully, "Mom, I just wish I could stand with Daniel on the corner one more time waiting for the school bus..." And then he left.

I sat down holding a cup of coffee in my trembling hands. Tears streamed down my face while sun danced on the table.

"God, it's funny what makes memories in the hearts of little children. You have given us such special children. Please help me never to neglect them because of the heavy demands of a handicapped child. *I WILL NEVER* again expect David and Becky to have the same level of commitment to their brother as Larry and I have."

And He, who knew all about heavy demands in His earthly ministry, seemed to whisper in my heart, "Oh?"

The "*I WILL NEVER...*" Chapter 31

(Or, "*I WILL NEVER* choose between hitting and hospitalization")

I glibly congratulated myself that we were doing well giving each child the attention he or she needed. Becky humbled me when she surprisingly related, "Momma, I hope Daniel hits me when he's home this weekend, 'cause then you're so nice to me."

I was shattered. I could not fathom that a child of mine was in such dire need of attention that she felt it worth the risk of being hurt.

The psychologist and social worker started family counseling in our home, preparing us for Dan's impending discharge on April 1st. We each had assigned seats around our kitchen table, and we each knew the rules.

Every family member, including Daniel, knew he was not ready for discharge.

The therapist suggested various ways of integrating our son back into our family life. "Perhaps," he offered, "he could dry the dishes." Little Becky chirped, "Oh, no, he couldn't do that. We just stick clean dishes in the sink and let them drain." The dishes in the plastic drainer in the sink behind her attested to her accuracy.

The psychologist pointedly asked Daniel, "Tell us why you'd like to live at home." I leaned back in the gold kitchen chair and relaxed a bit, confident our son had a clear-cut answer for that one. Flippantly, Dan mumbled, "I would like to live here because I like the view from the house."

I was destroyed. Larry was demolished. David and Becky puzzled.

The therapist pursued, "But, Dan, I live close to a golf course. It's beautiful where I live, but you wouldn't want to live with me." Dan quickly responded, "Oh, yes I sure would."

I found what I was hearing to be incredulous.

We prodded. We hinted. We all but said, "Repeat after me... 'I want to live at home because I love my family and they love me.'" Daniel refused to affirm any of it.

I wrote in my diary, "Rejection is hard to take. Where in the world did we fail?"

While Dan's aggression and self-abuse worsened at an alarming rate – yet the discharge date loomed closer – Larry and I discussed our fears. We both wallowed in guilt because of our fear and dread of Dan's living at home. Neither Daniel nor his family was ready.

The snows had melted, and the days were getting longer as crocuses tried to push their heads up through the stubborn, rich black soil by the parsonage door.

Larry drove me to the facility with unusual determination in his eyes. We soon sat on the edge of our chairs in this now familiar office. Larry spoke first, quickly and vehemently denouncing the pending discharge. With great emotion, he explained that Dan was worse than when he was hospitalized, and as head of our home, he would not allow our son to destroy us.

The whiskered psychologist leaned forward in his chair. The social worker quietly stared. I wondered if they were secretly thinking, "Aha. Hypocrites! For almost a year they have voiced their love for this child and now at the showdown, they are backing off."

I shuddered at the very thought. My eyes were fixed toward the dull, dusty floor, and I wanted to run.

The usually wordy therapist spoke succinctly, "You will have to decide, then, between having aggression at home or putting him in an institution for life. Your choice."

Strange. It sounded as simple as, "French fries or baked potato? Soup or salad? Aggression at home or institutionalization? Choose one."

The man directed his next question to me. "Jane, are your prepared to make that choice?" The question was superfluous. They cared not whether I was prepared. I was being forced to choose.

Three people stared at me, waiting for a response. I tried to ignore the gapes in my direction as I agonized inside. I could literally hear the office clock ticking in the deafening silence. For ten months I had been nobly restrained in this office, my emotions carefully checked. I was proud of my emotional track record.

But this time, the lid blew.

Hysterically, I railed, "How do you have the nerve to ask a mother that? This child has destroyed two parsonages. He has seriously hurt every family member. We have done everything we know to help. But we love him with all our being. We can't just 'put him away'. How can you make me choose?" I sobbed loudly into my hands. I'd never heard such sounds since giving birth.

The social worker handed me a tissue although everyone continued to stare and speak not a word.

In my anguish I inwardly speculated, "They've waited for ten months to see me crack. I hope they're satisfied. They are probably clapping on the inside." When everyone realized this was more difficult for me than they had anticipated, Larry and I left.

Larry brought in hamburgers for supper and cued David and Becky not to ask any questions of me.

Alone in the evening, I prayed, "Father, there is no alternative. Surely, You don't want him in an institution for life. And surely You don't want him hurting us. There is no other option but that You heal his brain. Have You been waiting for us to be this desperate? *I WILL NEVER* be more desperate."

And He soothed my heart and seemed to ask, "Oh?"

The "*I WILL NEVER...*" Chapter 32

(Or, "*I WILL NEVER* stay in the ministry")

Dan was not healed.

Larry and I met an expert in the field of behavior modification, and Larry, with new hope in his heart, cheerily greeted the educator, "Hello. So you're the BM expert."

Taken back by Larry's greeting, the expert stoically explained, "Behavior modification is used in the treatment of behavior disorders through the application of positive reinforcements for the desired behavior and lack of positive reinforcements for undesirable behavior."

Rewards and loss of rewards pretty well sums that up.

It was only a few weeks before the staff realized they were too weary after a year of intensive treatment with little progress to effectively implement the time-consuming behavior modification program. The professionals searched for a new facility that specialized in this approach.

A change would be refreshing.

I had balked each time we had filled out the pass to take Dan off grounds. The pass contained Dan's patient number, birthday, and a place to note any scratches or bruises *before* he left the grounds – and a place to note any *new* marks, scratches, or bruises *after* he returned from a visit. I detested what that implied.

Daniel was never free of injuries. Black and swollen eyes were common. Two broken, jagged front teeth often pierced his lip. While *he* received none of these at home, *we* received many injuries, although there was no place to document them on the pass.

Larry once again dutifully signed the pass and took Dan to a nearby motel to swim. It was bitterly cold and sleeting, but the motel had offered their heated indoor pool for Dan's use. After an uneventful swim, Larry was helping Daniel get dressed in the small dressing room. Dan became violent, and Larry restricted him to a chair.

Larry hurriedly tried to get himself dressed when he glanced in the mirror and saw his son behind him with a raised shoe, ready to strike him in the head. As Larry turned to deflect it, his elbow hit Dan's chin causing his lip to begin to bleed. Daniel became totally unmanageable while Larry tried to gather wet towels, wet suits, a hair dryer, as well as get a bleeding, flailing boy into his coat, boots, and hat to brave the blizzard outside.

They rode in a crowded elevator in this luxurious hotel while formally attired partygoers gaped at them as chlorine leaked onto the floor through the wet paper bag holding their belongings. Larry later mentioned it seemed to be a very long ride to the lobby.

Driving back to the facility, Larry was shaken, angry, embarrassed, worried, and tired. He whisked Dan to the door, cuddling him against the blizzard and pressing his handkerchief against Dan's lip while waiting for the door to be unlocked. Daniel screamed wildly.

The staff interrogated my husband at length, looking for inconsistencies. Larry felt humiliated by their probing questions and raised eyebrows.

Larry came home defeated in heart. Beaten. Whipped.

"No time to hurt now, Larry. We're due over at the church in thirty minutes for a concert," I cautioned unsympathetically.

Several days later, the same staff called and reported that Daniel had mysteriously hurt his head while serving a restriction and needed stitches. Larry was tempted to drill them for answers as they had done to him. But he refrained.

A new facility was finally located only two hours away in Champaign, Illinois. We all – Larry, Jane, Dan, and worn-out staff – knew it was time for Daniel to move on.

Next door at the church, however, there were "rumblings in the camp."

The pastor and the people realized we could no longer continue to minister there. The church needed a minister who was refreshed. Larry spent three days a week visiting and being counseled in a mental institution, as well as being abused by his own son each weekend. This pastor had depleted emotions, a broken spirit, and a heaviness of heart that would not go away.

Larry agonized over the decision to resign. He loved expounding the Word of God there. But the people needed more than we could give, and with great reluctance my husband tendered his resignation.

The Bateman family had no salary and no place to go. After several months of our renting the parsonage from the church, a surprising letter from the board demanded a $400 security deposit on the parsonage and $800 a month rent until we found a place to live.

Larry explained we had no income, and since the church had not located another minister, we did not understand the security deposit nor the $400 increase in rent.

A letter from the chairman of the board curtly stated, "Please make the necessary arrangements to vacate the premises in two weeks; we shall be on hand on that date to repossess our facility."

I sat in the chaise lounge in the warm sun, clutching the mail. Kicking my shoes off, I leaned my head back against the chair and prayed out loud, "Father, how can Christians behave this way? *I WILL NEVER* understand the brethren!" I sighed, realizing I needed to start packing to vacate these "premises" for an "undisclosed location."

I continued venting, "I have reached my limit. *I WILL NEVER* remain in ministry."

And He, who knows all about the brethren (and the "sistern") seemed to say, "Oh?"

The "*I WILL NEVER...*" Chapter 33

(Or, "*I WILL NEVER* forget Champaign and McDonalds")

Big purple doors opened to Dan's homey cottage in his new place in Champaign, Illinois. I liked the sound of "cottage" so much more than unit.

After signing papers and getting Daniel situated into his very own private room, it was time to say good-bye.

Realizing we had never been so far away from this dear little boy, my quivering lips could only pucker for a kiss. Words would not come.

I handed my son his bag of candy and ran out of the purple doors to our car. Larry and I drove slowly down the winding roads to the main highway. Tears would not stop. I finally broke the silence. "Larry, they were giving him soup for lunch. He can't eat soup without help because of his paralyzed hand. Should I have told them he needs someone to hold the bowl?"

After our two-hour drive we reached the parsonage and immediately began packing for a move to nowhere.

Wrapping glasses in newspaper, I nagged, "Larry, please go find secular work. Families in the ministry live in a fish bowl, and our struggling family cannot measure up to scrutiny. Our time and energy are sapped with Daniel with no reserves for the ministry. Please, let's get out."

Larry mutely kept packing until my whining eventually wound down.

"Jane Lee," he thoughtfully began, "I was called by God to the ministry. I cannot just leave it because a few people hurt our feelings. Jane, this is my calling. Do you understand? My calling." His eyes pierced my soul. "I thought this was your calling, too," he added.

I began packing books faster. "Honey," I began in candy-heart tones, "I don't mind the ministry, as such, but *I WILL NEVER* want you to pastor again. Why not look around for another type of ministry?"

I felt better.

Several days later a Christian organization interviewed us and offered a position. While the new job brought a measure of security, we still did not know *where* we would serve with the organization.

We left that week for a brief respite at Ben Lippen Bible Conference in Asheville, North Carolina, although we needed to be out of the parsonage two days after we returned. During our brief time at the conference, I felt misplaced. Unsure. Lonely. Homeless. I was oozing with fresh open wounds.

God provided us the privilege of having lunch with Dr. Vance Havner, the conference speaker for the week. Seated at a large, round table with the mountains visible through the windows, Dr. Havner intently listened to our situation. We leaned in to hear his every word as he whispered in his slow, Southern drawl, "This'll either make you bitter or better."

141

Larry and I climbed along a narrow path up a steep hill. I pulled my sweater around me as we sat on a bench in the night mountain air. Larry put one arm around me and held my hand as we prayed together, "Lord, we'll go anywhere."

Larry and I embraced as I silently added, "*I WILL NEVER* cease to trust you.*"

And in the stillness He, who had no place to lay His head during His time on earth, seemed to ask in my heart, "Oh?"

The "*I WILL NEVER...*" Chapter 34

(Or, "*I WILL NEVER* store my stuff")

"*I WILL NEVER* store my furniture. I love it. I dust it. I keep people's feet off of it." I proclaimed. But store it we did.

It was a humid, muggy night in a midwestern state as we marched down the long, echoing halls of a training center to live in a stark dormitory-style setting.

I could think of nothing worse for David and Becky. Dormitory life lacked security for a son entering his teens while our little girl entered first grade. I told God I felt He was making a colossal mistake. I mentioned it to Larry a time or two as well.

I felt scattered. My furniture was retained in a warehouse in Illinois. Daniel was hospitalized in another part of the state. Larry's books rested in Indiana. And we were living in yet another state in a bleak, sterile building while being trained in our new ministry.

I sat in our tiny room, peering through the one window. The plain floor and the two pieces of furniture – a bed and desk – were as drab as our parsonages had been plush. The women's bathroom was on another floor, the men's closer.

After pouring our souls into the intensive training, we drove five hours every other weekend to be with Daniel. He seemed so content in his new facility, yet he screamed each time we left.

Because we had classes on Thanksgiving, we could not be with Daniel. We all huddled in the phone booth at the end of our hall to talk to him. He brokenly said, "Momma, I'm the only kid here. Everybody else went home."

That will ring in my heart as long as I live.

Becky needed her adenoids out and tubes put in her ears. It was a frigid day as she and I drove to the hospital.
I was alone in a large unfamiliar city, fifty miles away from our dormitory. I knew not a soul. I had never met the doctor. I had no family close by. Larry was out of town seeking a place of service after our graduation in one week from our training. I had not realized being in a hospital again with a sick child would trigger so many memories.

I lay awake on a hospital cot next to the petite sleeping first-grader. The hall light creeping under the door danced along the dark floor, looking dismal and hopeful at the same time.

The door opened quietly, and the hall light reflected on the worn face of my husband. He excitedly whispered that we would be moving to Springfield, Illinois to minister. He had even found a house to rent.

Larry kissed me, kissed his sleeping daughter, and left to go back to the training center where David was. I snuggled under the rough hospital sheet, content.

A week later our proud children looked on as Larry and I "pomped and circumstanced" down the aisle with the rest of our graduating classmates. It seemed I had spent the entire three months caring for a sick daughter and traveling to and from Illinois to visit Daniel.

I lay in bed that night, surrounded by boxes and one wilting plant. I reflected on how I had resisted coming to this very place. I silently prayed, "Lord, this place was exactly what we needed after we left the pastorate. We needed this cocoon of love. Where else could Becky have raised a butterfly? Where else could she have made close friends with children from other countries? Where else could David have celebrated his thirteenth birthday with toilet paper strewn across a dining hall door, cutting the paper to the delight of a large group of people? Thank you, Father."

It was a sad day for all the Batemans as we bade farewell to newfound friends. Worming our way down the long driveway to the highway, I whispered to the Lord, "*I WILL NEVER* doubt your wisdom again."

And, He, who knew what lay just around the corner, seemed to say in my heart, "Oh?"

The "*I WILL NEVER...*" Chapter 35

(Or, "*I WILL NEVER* beg for my husband's help")

Our nomadic family relaxed in the dining room of the rented home. Larry joyfully explained that the owner had taken down the "for sale" sign and promised us a whole year in the house before trying to sell it.

It felt good to have a place.

Not since we had left Virginia almost two years earlier had I felt so settled.

Three weeks later, the landlord brought a couple through the house "just to look at it." I thought nothing about his simplistic statement.

Christmas brought a new puppy, a two-day visit from Daniel, and dangerous aggressions. He threw the Christmas tree and choked the puppy. The family fared no better. There were a few tender moments, however, as the three children hung old drapes in the basement and acted out the Christmas story. The stench left by a new puppy added just the right touch to the barnyard scene.

On New Year's Eve we watched a children's special on television. I watched with a happy heart, knowing Dan was watching the same special in his facility. I peered out of the window to watch the ice storm swirl about our "little house on the prairie" and laid the afghan on my feet.

My cozy feeling was interrupted by the telephone. The staff in Champaign apologetically revealed that Daniel had slipped out in the storm with neither shoes nor coat on. The police were summoned and had eventually found him in some nearby apartment buildings.

Snow by the buckets-full made travel to our son almost impossible, and I complained, "Lord, you have brought us near and yet not near enough to get to him. That's cruel." There were times, in desperation to get to him, we were the only vehicle on the road. These foolish Southerners were rushing out where even Midwesterners feared to tread.

Bringing Daniel back in the car with us every other weekend produced life-threatening situations. Larry and I had to don protective gear in order to arrive unscathed.

Larry protected his hair from being pulled by wearing a wool cap pulled down over his ears. Even in July. I wore a matching one for the same reason. We both wore turtlenecks to protect our necks from being clawed. Larry taped his glasses to his head to keep Daniel from quickly grabbing them and hurling them out of the open car window (Becky once told me one of her favorite childhood memories was looking for her Daddy's glasses in the median strip of the interstate).

One of the caseworkers suggested putting gloves on Daniel and then covering them with oven mitts so he could not pinch or scratch. That proved to be somewhat effective, although he was like Houdini, escaping from the mitts more often than not. We used the leftover tape from Larry's glasses to wrap around a tongue depressor that rested on the seat belt buckle release, hoping the wooden depressor would keep Daniel from pushing the button and escaping from his seat belt. Sometimes it worked. Sometimes it did not.

The psychologist, bless him, suggested Larry and I switch drivers halfway home. Larry often wrapped Dan mummy-style in a blanket to prevent self-abuse. Meanwhile, I floored the accelerator, secretly hoping a policeman would pull me over. I had my speech prepared, "Thank you, sir. You take him the rest of the way."

I giggled at times at the stares from people in other cars, wondering if anyone had taken down our license plate number to call the police regarding a probable kidnapping. Their report would sound authentic:

> *Woman in strange hat exceeding speed limit –*
> *Man, disguised with strange hat pulled down on head*
> *A struggling child wrapped in a blanket*
> *Man has white tape holding glasses on*

One evening as we attempted to return Dan to the facility, he grabbed his bedspread, his beloved flag off his wall, and pleaded, "Please don't take me back." The ensuing struggle made us late for our departure. After our usual two-hour harrowing trip to the cottage, we arrived fifteen minutes later than usual to find this note tacked by the staff on the locked cottage door: "Gone to movies with all the kids. Be back at 8."

Through quick investigative work on our part, our task of finding the staff and children was not a difficult one.

The popcorn smell invaded the darkness of the theatre while I asked a uniformed man, swinging a flashlight, if he knew of a group of children there from a mental health facility. He seemed to know them well. Daniel and I, suitcase in hand, made our way to the front (of course) to join the group.

Let's just say the staff was not as joyful to see Daniel, as he was to see them.

As I left, I could envision parents nearby asking what kind of a mother brought her kid to the movie with a suitcase.

Home visits continued to be horrendous, and I felt desperate guilt over my dread of them. Hanging my head in remorse, I explained my feelings to the therapist working with our family. He inquired, "Who looks forward to being pinched, kicked, and bitten each weekend? Who do you think you are – the Virgin Mary?"

Friction was evident in our family during Dan's home visits. The staff instructed Larry not to assist me during my struggles with our son unless I specifically invited him, nor was I to interfere with Larry's interactions with Daniel unless I was asked. I hated the rule, feeling unprotected. It was humbling to admit I needed help. "*I WILL NEVER* beg for help," I stubbornly affirmed.

It was late on a Friday evening. We had just entered our house after the long trek. Daniel was as determined to gouge out his eye as I was determined that he would not. I struggled with him on the living room floor, loosing the battle in restraining his hand. Although we had been taught pressure points in order to restrain, I could not let go of Dan's finger pushing hard on his eye to find a pressure point. Terror gripped my heart. Larry sat in a chair observing, obediently following our treatment plan. Furious, I screeched hysterically, "Help me!"

Larry threw himself on the floor and held Dan in a tight grasp as I fled to the bathroom. Behind the locked door, I moaned, "I cannot stand another minute of this. God, you must heal him now. I demand it! I claim it."

I could not sleep that night. My eyes stared at the ceiling as an occasional light from a passing car reflected against it. It was nearing dawn when I whispered, "Father, I am so weary. Please take me to heaven. *I WILL NEVER* endure this grief."

And He, whose strength is made perfect in weakness, seemed to say in my heart, "Oh?"

The "*I WILL NEVER...*" Chapter 36

(Or, "*I WILL NEVER* allow Becky to suffer...")

Becky made the ultimate sacrifice.

The six year old smiled at her ten-year-old brother and cooed, "Dan, when Momma and Daddy drive you back to Champaign tonight, I want to go too."

At that, Dan hurled a large, heavy chair from the top of the stairs as she stood in the narrow stairwell. Screaming, she clung to the wall as the chair whisked by her head.

Larry struggled to get Daniel down the steps and into the bathroom for time-out while I held Becky. Scenes flashed of an earlier time when he had tried to hold her head under the water in a pool. As I held her close, I railed, "God, I can see how you could allow such trials in my life. And even in Larry's life. But how can you allow this in a little girl's life? She will probably hate men the rest of her life. She'll never trust anyone. You are making a terrible mistake."

As I sheltered my pixie daughter in my arms, she turned her eyes to meet mine. She whispered, "Momma, you know

151

when Daniel grows up – if he is not well and nobody wants him, I'll marry him."

I could almost hear the Father asking, "Now will you trust me in your children's lives? Do you see the quality of love she's learned? Do you think she could have learned it any other way?"

As I squeezed tightly this little one who had seen so much struggle in her young life, I rested my chin on her golden hair.

"*I WILL NEVER* need such dramatic reassurances of Your workings in my children's lives again."

And He, who knows about tough and tender love, seemed to ask in my heart, "Oh?"

The "*I WILL NEVER...*" Chapter 37

(Or, "*I WILL NEVER* be Your replica")

I was livid with rage when our landlord sheepishly announced he had sold the house to the couple to which he had shown it twenty-two days after we had unpacked.

We sat around the kitchen table, Larry vainly searching for the right words to explain our situation to our children. David's reaction blurted forth, "I'm not going to another school this year!" David and Becky were dreading going to their third school that year, and it was only February.

In his wistful way David strung his lanky legs over the chair and sighed, "I just want to say I was raised somewhere."

Several days later, David, pale and shaky, opened the back door for his Daddy and me. He rapidly explained, "A sheriff's car drove up in our driveway. I thought you all had been killed on the road from Champaign and he was coming to tell me. I hid Becky in the bathroom so I could break the news to her myself. But he just handed me these papers."

Eviction papers had been served to our thirteen-year-old son. He had skirted the legal jargon and understood the meat of the notice, which he summarized in shotgun fashion for us.

We had been evicted from the parsonage and now evicted from a rental house? What in the world...?

After moving into our little white, Cape Cod home in the capital of Illinois, our new neighbors paid a friendly visit. Daniel was also visiting, and it was difficult to be conversational, not knowing how safe their son was in the playroom with Daniel. When he tried to hurl the coffee table, Larry restrained him, and our new neighbors – who had come to get acquainted – quickly left. Come to think of it, I don't remember their ever coming back.

The entire month was a bad one. Daniel had said, "I'll kill myself if it's the last thing I do." He had pulled a butcher knife on us; had to be restrained in the back seat of our Volkswagen bug for two hours; stabbed his beloved math tutor in the chest with a pencil; and broke Larry's glasses (yet again).

We learned too that after "lights out" in the cottage a group of patients grabbed belts and entered Dan's room, beating him as he slept. Later at a staff meeting, someone asked the staff, "If it were totally dark, who would be the one kid on the unit in most danger of reprisal by the other kids?" There was no doubt but that it would be Daniel.

Hints of discouragement seeped into the staff's voices. They began using words like "burnt out."

Technically, Daniel belonged in a mental health facility closer to our home. We loved the present facility and did not want to change. We were seeing some improvement in our son, and the staff treated us with dignity, something we had sorely missed in the other institutions.

The stunning lady psychologist, in a denim suit and red heels, explained that because neither drugs nor behavior modification techniques were having the desired results, she had another option. Realizing the love Dan had for his family, she wanted to capitalize on that and have him earn home visits by good behavior. Larry and I balked at holding family time as a club over Dan's head.

We tried to explain grace and justice, as we perceived them. We wanted visits home to be a picture of grace to our son while justice was taught another way. Our words sounded hollow. Our theology sounded fuzzy.

We reluctantly agreed to the new treatment plan, and Daniel did not come home for three weeks. When he earned a visit home, he immediately went into our bedroom and donned Larry's suit coat and limped into the living room. The extended sleeves dangling over his arms, the long coat brushing his jeans, he moaned, "Daddy, all I want is to be just like you. That's all I want in my whole life."

There he stood.

So much potential wasted.

The intelligent brain in an old man's body.

Daddy's replica – all broken.

I gingerly helped Daniel out of the over-sized coat. Soothing his aching heart, I invited him into the kitchen. I choked back salty tears as I watched him labor over a bowl of Jell-O.

I stirred a pot on the stove and recycled Dan's plea in my heart, "Daddy, all I want is to be just like you. That's all I want..."

And I prayed, "Father, I just want to be like you. I know I am 'clothed' in your righteousness, but so often the sleeves dangle. *I WILL NEVER* be your replica to a lost world."

And He, who cloaked me with His righteousness, seemed to ask in my heart, "Oh?"

The "*I WILL NEVER...*" Chapter 38

(Or, "*I WILL NEVER* again inflict pain")

Larry and I sat in the office on the small sofa, the cushions sagging a bit above the stained carpet. A dim table lamp was used when the fluorescent one in the ceiling flickered. The bearded psychologist leaned forward. In low tones he said, "Daniel is totally absorbed with himself. He needs to realize that other family members are hurting too. I want you to tell Dan what you both have lost since his injury."

I recoiled, feeling unprepared for my "pop quiz." I felt we would be treating Daniel much like someone had described a battered politician: "Here is someone washed up on our shore with both arms broken, both legs broken, and now we are asked to cut off his head and rip out his heart."

The little drooling boy dressed in a tank top, cut offs, and tennis shoes was ushered into the room. He was excited to see his parents in the middle of the week and gazed up at me with trusting eyes. I did not want to betray that trust by placing an adult-sized pain in his tender, hurting heart.

The professional nodded for me to begin. I hesitated.

After taking a deep breath, I stuttered – "Daniel, you know, I remember the doctor giving me good news of a new baby coming. And I remember how you looked the day you were born. I remember long curls and dimples. And fat cheeks Daddy lovingly and tenderly pinched."

I paused. Even the sweet memories were painful. A knot had crawled into my throat, and I swallowed before I continued. "I remember strawberries each year on your birthday cake – and trips where you were our best traveler. I remember you painting pictures with shaving cream in kindergarten."

Daniel smiled as we relived happier times.

I patted his hand and continued, "And I remember the expression on your face the first time you held your baby sister. I remember how proud you were of new Easter shoes. And, of course, how you were always the earliest riser on Christmas morning."

Dan giggled, knowing he was the early riser every morning.

The words flowed easier now, "I remember you learning to ride a bike. Remember how fast you wanted to go? I remember that special day when you asked Jesus into your heart – do you remember calling Grandma and telling her?" He remembered.

"Dan," I recalled, "I remember how you loved the circus. And Myrtle Beach – you were the bravest rider in the amusement park. I remember your expression as you looked at Daddy when he baptized you. And then I wrapped the towel around you and told you how much you were loved.

Through quivering lips, you said, 'I love you, too.'" I paused. I did not want to go on.

The psychologist, cracking his knuckles, motioned for me to continue.

I stammered, "I remember one Sunday night you wiggled in church. You wrote me a love note and then carefully copied the words on the communion table: 'Do this in remembrance of Me.' I still have that note. Do you remember suggesting we sing your favorite hymn that night? You bellowed, 'I Shall Not Be Moved' in your seven-year-old voice. I remember we drove home and marched around your room with David and Becky pretending to be soldiers. And then after kissing you and David, I tucked David in the bottom bunk and you into the top bunk. As I turned out the light, I whispered, 'I love you, David and Daniel.'"

I abruptly ceased talking. Recalling those memories that seemed to have happened in another lifetime was excruciating. Tears streamed down my neck. Dan was whimpering beside me, drooling profusely.

The psychologist coldly instructed, "Mrs. Bateman, tell him what you've lost!"

Having safely guarded my despondent feelings for several years, I was not sure I wanted to risk exposure now. Breathing shallowly, I reluctantly resumed, "After I tucked you in bed that night, my life changed."

Daniel sobbed loudly. Wailed.

I strangled – blew my nose – and grabbed Larry's hand. I pleaded with the therapist, "Please let me stop now."

The professional again motioned for me to continue.

"Daniel," I persisted, "I miss you. I feel I'm losing you. I want to raise you and watch you grow. I want to have a major role in your life. Dan, it hurts me to see you struggling to

159

walk and talk. But it hurts far worse when you hit me. I just want to be your mom and cook for you and see you off each morning to school..." I buried my face in my hands, weeping uncontrollably.

Daniel had tried to bolt from the room several times as I was speaking. He knew, as did I, that my dreams were out of reach. I sat close to the edge of the tattered sofa and nervously shredded my tissue.

Undaunted, though moved, the psychologist asked Larry to relate to Dan what he had lost since his son had fallen.

Larry found it difficult to upbraid his beloved son with "see-what's-happened-to-our-family-because-of-you" speech. With thick emotion already pervading the small room, Larry spoke briefly. Weeping softly, he told Daniel how he had longed to teach him daily the marvelous truths of God; how he had longed to watch Dan apply those truths in his life; how he had looked forward, since Dan's birth, to his growing into a man of God, as was his Biblical namesake. He then admonished Daniel concerning the severity with which God deals with children who strike their parents.

The emotions melted into silence. The psychologist was visibly shaken as the three Batemans held each other tightly and wept.

We kissed Dan good-bye and walked slowly down the hall. I had a gnawing, secret urge to apologize to my son for hurting him, but I knew the therapist would never allow that.

On the ride home Larry and I blankly stared at the straight, flat roads, the Illinois countryside yielding its corn on both sides. We did not speak. We had filibustered earlier, and we reveled in the silence.

I closed my eyes against the sun sinking in the west. "God, I know you willingly afflicted your beloved Son in my place, and it hurt you. *I WILL NEVER* loose sight of the fact that you know what parental agony is all about."

And the Son, who had been forsaken by His Father, seemed to say in my heart, "Oh?"

The "*I WILL NEVER...*" Chapter 39

(Or, "*I WILL NEVER* be a visual aid to my children")

Daniel's claim to fame, as he saw it, was his falling from the top bunk. His aggressions accelerated when another patient was admitted because he too had fallen from a top bunk.

In early October I drove alone to Champaign. The two staff sat in the familiar small room with me at the facility. I was nervous because Larry was not with me and I chewed my gum faster than was necessary. The session was a heated one. The staff concluded that I was angry with God, and Daniel was just expressing *my* anger. Furthermore, I was assured I could not be human were I not angry.

One staff horrified me as she stated, "And frankly, I wouldn't want to live in your house either." The implication that our son chose not to live with us sliced through my very being.

I deposited my gum into a tissue and, in vain, tried to argue my case. I was defensive and handled my presentation poorly. I mumbled something about my strong desire to be a visual aid of God's unconditional love to Dan. The staff quickly countered, "You can't be a picture of God to your children because you are mortal."

I tried to explain, but I could almost hear their thoughts: "Don't try to give us answers. You're the family with the problems. You came to us. We did not come to you."

I sat stunned. My body shivered. I wondered how to explain to deaf ears what I believed and would die for.

Hypnotically, my eyes stared at the road as I drove home. Out loud I questioned, "Lord, am I really angry with you and don't even know it? Can't I still be a picture to our children of your love even though I'm human? Oh, dear God, please give me some answers...I am so confused."

Larry was painting the basement when I arrived home. The moist, cool air hit my wet face while I poured out the details of my meeting with staff. Larry put down his brush and held me.

"Jane, is it your *heart* – or the *staff* – making you feel uneasy?" my husband wisely asked.

I sat on the bare basement floor and watched Larry dip the brush in light green paint. After a lengthy silence, I thoughtfully began, "Larry, I believe that long ago we both worked through any anger we had toward God. Perhaps it resurfaces from time to time, but I believe – as far as I know my heart – I am not angry because of what God has allowed in our lives."

Slathering the paint on the wall, Larry smiled at me over his shoulder.

I skipped up the steps into the kitchen.

I joyfully attacked the dirty dishes and prayed, "Father, I know it would be natural to be angry. But I want my life to be supernatural. *I WILL NEVER* rest until my life is full of the supernatural working of God."

And He, who knows my growth is not always consistent, seemed to ask in my heart, "Oh?"

The "*I WILL NEVER...*" Chapter 40

(Or, "*I WILL NEVER* play Tackle Frisbee again")

Excited, Larry set up a flannel board in our living room for a special Bible lesson with Daniel. As Larry had studied during the week, he had eagerly remarked, "Dan will just love this Bible lesson...he'll just love it."

Within minutes Dan ripped all the visuals, broke the board, and hurled it across the room. Devastated and disappointed, Larry gathered up the shredded pieces and cried.

Early Monday morning, the social worker in Champaign called me. Sadness ruled her voice as she tried to break the news gently, "Jane, if we had a cottage just for Daniel and a whole fresh army of staff, we could manage. But, of course, we have neither. We just can no longer service Dan. I'm sorry. Really sorry."

I could sense how defeated she felt. She and others had poured their hearts into our son.

I did not realize just how worn the staff was until our next visit to the facility. We arrived early Saturday morning to take Dan to McDonalds and to a mall crowded with weekend shoppers. Activities are limited with an explosive child. When Daniel became threatening (meaning a fist or foot aimed in our direction without bodily contact) during this outing, we returned quickly to the residential facility. Larry and the children sat in the car while I ran into the cottage to request the key to the gym. Two staff lashed out, "You may not use the gym. We want you to keep him off these grounds until 5 p.m. Lady, we are tired and burnt out!"

I was enraged. The gym was on another part of the grounds – not even close to the cottage – and I was incensed with their response. My set jaws barely moved as I said in iced tones, "I can see you are burnt out."

SO ARE WE.

I tried to diffuse my anger before I reached my weary family waiting in the car.

I slipped into the back seat and quietly announced, "We need to think of something to do for the next two hours, folks..." Larry's eyes glared in the rearview mirror at mine in total disbelief.

We found a park and played Frisbee and football. When 5 p.m. *finally* arrived, our tackle football and tackle Frisbee games ended. Dan had done all the tackling, and we were anxious to return to the cottage.

I reported the staff's behavior to their supervisor, and she responded,

> *Their conduct was most unprofessional. I will tell them again; this is a mental health facility, not a prep school for Harvard.*

She said that often, and I smiled every time.

It was on a special Thanksgiving "date" with his beloved staff, Linda, when Daniel adamantly asserted, "I'm not leaving her. Ever."

But on November 24, a hesitant Linda met us at the purple doors. Dan's suitcases were quickly loaded while Linda busied herself. Kisses and hugs were exchanged. I had a "we-will-never-forget-the-part-you've-played-in-our-lives" speech prepared, but I could not manage any words.

The car slowly pulled away, leaving the beaten, bruised, and discouraged staff gently waving.

"I'll miss the staff – and especially Linda. But *I WILL NEVER* miss these horrible seventy mile rides every weekend."

A toasty feeling warmed my heart, realizing Dan belonged to us exclusively for the weekend before being admitted to a mental health center close to our home in Springfield. We had his clothes, his toys, and the fellow himself under our roof.

"Father," I prayed after all three children were tucked in bed, "the five Batemans are together. *I WILL NEVER* forget how good it feels to have all my children under one roof."

The next morning when Daniel tore down the drapes, God seemed to say, "Oh?"

The "*I WILL NEVER...*" Chapter 41

(Or, "*I WILL NEVER* sit and stare at a therapist")

The patient photographer got us "switchuated," as Becky would say. The frozen smiles revealed our uncertainties about Dan's standing closely behind us and beside us. Daniel earned his ice cream cone for good behavior, and the rest of us earned one for bravery.

The next morning Larry stayed home with his son while the other children went to church with me. The ringing phone in the church kitchen startled me. Instinctively, I knew it was for me. Larry cursively detailed how he had been bathing Dan, and when he had helped him out of the bathtub, Dan had taken a swing at his Dad. Daniel lost his balance and cut his head in the tub. Larry asked me to meet him at the hospital.

Dan calmly lay on the table in the emergency room, enjoying patient status. As the doctor cleansed the wound, Dan asked, "So, doc, how's your love life?" Larry glanced at me, and I returned an anemic smile.

Dan was up the next morning at 4 a.m., anxious to go to his new "place." He propelled a trashcan at me when I told him it was too early to go anywhere.

Again, the suitcase and bags of toys were packed. I knew the day would be filled with new papers to sign that seemed to document our need for help and that seemed to accentuate our inadequacy. There would be a new set of old questions. There would be the re-living of the story – again – to a new social worker. There would be questions reeking in our hearts about how much to "cue" new staff. There would be meeting new emotionally disturbed children and becoming acquainted with a new routine. There would be the awkward feeling of trying to assure staff that this patient's family loved him and that he was being admitted because there was no other alternative.

A kind lady with brown curly hair warmly welcomed Daniel to his cheery room. As I carefully placed his clothes into his dresser, she sat much too near Dan on the bed. She patted him, and I watched cautiously, lest he return her "pat."

One optimistic staff commented, "He's the sweetest boy. You just can't be mad at him." I was tempted to request that she record that so I could play it back in several weeks (she quit work several months later).

Daniel took the green, seedless grapes we had brought and walked into the television area. He looked small and vulnerable in such large halls.

I kept my eyes straight ahead. *I guess one never gets used to admitting one's child to a mental institution. But I thought this time it would be a little easier. Wonder how come it's always so hard...*

In anguish, Larry and I left.

The new therapist soon reported Daniel tried to break his glasses, and with that bit of news, I decided my son was settling into his new environment.

Terror struck my heart as the therapist informed us that he wanted to meet weekly with Larry and me – separately. I was shaken because I had trusted Larry to verbalize what I felt. I never had to "solo" before, and I did not like the thought of my co-pilot being ejected suddenly; I was not sure how well I would soar.

Larry met with the psychologist first and warned me that he was not of the talkative variety. As I entered his office, I wore my most secure smile and my most "emotionally stable" look. I held my head staunchly aloft while I peered at the papers strewn about the small room. A struggling plant in front of the large window looked as weary from struggling as I felt. An orange macramé hanger tried to brighten one wall. Trying to be conversational, I said something about macramé. Just how long can someone talk about macramé?

Awkward silence permeated the room. My mind skipped back to college and my get-acquainted conference with the dean. Having said, "Welcome, Jane Lee," she leaned back in her chair and smiled. The silence that followed screamed at me to talk. I babbled for an hour, revealing morsels in my life I never intended to reveal to anyone – much less the dean.

I determined not to be as emotionally vulnerable with this therapist. Nervously fidgeting with my purse, the secret fear taunted me that if I stopped talking after 15 minutes, the therapist would stare at me for the next 45. Maybe I could just raise my hand and asked to be excused?

I did all right at the first session (But on subsequent visits I took in prepared speeches, later just outlines, and finally mere notes. My "extemperaneousity" would not fail).

After the first session I slowly walked down the long, unfamiliar hall to Dan's room. As I rounded the corner, I recognized my son's hysterical screams. Seated on the bed next to Dan, a young staff comforted me, "Sometimes a homesick boy just needs his mother." I liked this staff member.

Dan mourned inconsolably – realizing how closely he now lived to home – and how far he actually was.

When his cries stopped temporarily for supper, I pulled my coat collar up around my ears and left in the cold, dark night. Although my fingers stung on the frigid steering wheel, the real sting was deep in my heart. Driving to another city to speak at a church gathering, I began praying, "Father, comfort my hurting boy and give me a desire to speak tonight because it's the last thing on earth I want to do." I rehearsed my devotional in my mind, "God Uses Broken Things," and asked God to make the message fresh to me as I spoke.

The church was decorated festively for Christmas. My heart was dull – unfestive. After shaking hands with friendly ladies, I took my seat. The altos and sopranos blended to soothe my heart as they sang the last verse of "Away in a Manger."

> *Be near me, Lord Jesus, I ask Thee to stay*
> *Close by me forever, and love me, I pray*
> *Bless all the dear children in Thy tender care*
> *And take us to Heaven to live with Thee there.*

Silently I prayed, "Father, I sure wish 'thy tender care' were more visible. *I WILL NEVER* get used to this trusting without any obvious results."

As I rose to walk to the podium to speak, He, who uses broken things, seemed to ask in my heart, "Oh?

The "*I WILL NEVER...*" Chapter 42

(Or, "*I WILL NEVER* forget the ungluing")

I stood in the toy store amidst the other holiday shoppers. The usual grumbling was evident. Mothers looked weary. Fathers, agitated. Parents did not always agree on the perfect purchase, and "just-wait-till-we-get-home" glances were exchanged.

I rested my hands on my empty cart and drowned in my sea of misery. I prepared a silent speech I wanted to shout to the murmuring: "Parents, LISTEN UP. Do you have any idea how hard it is to buy for a boy with only one hand that works? To buy a toy that he cannot injure others with? Do you know what it's like to have a list of requests from your child and know he cannot play with any of them? Do you know what it's like to buy the 'perfect' gift – only to have it returned by staff because it was used as a weapon? So, stop complaining. In other words, shut up."

I admit that was not one of my better moments but I did feel better after I mulled over my muted speech.

Taking a deep breath, I wove my empty cart around brimming ones pushed by grumbling parents.

I prayed, "Father, *I WILL NEVER* look forward to Christmas ever again."

I parked my empty cart and quietly left the busy store after making no purchases.

A three-foot dollhouse, painstakingly erected by Larry and David, stood tall in the dining room. Becky's eyes brightened, and her patience wore thin as the architects spent hours assembling her wonderland. Because the "real working elevator" never really worked, much less elevated, the new tiny plastic lady of the house just decided to use the plastic steps. Miniature furniture was arranged and rearranged carefully by delicate eight-year-old hands.

When Daniel visited us on Christmas Day, he stumbled, crashed on the dollhouse, and the "walls came a-tumbling down." Amazing how much faster this cardboard residence went down than it had gone up.

Everyone cried – the crasher who had just "dropped in," the little girl who "owned" the smashed house, and the weary construction workers.

That night, I wrote in my diary, "I took a terrible picture of Larry tonight. He had a large bottle of glue and was 'epoxily' doctoring Becky's dollhouse. His face shows disappointment and disgust and determination. It is pouring rain, and water is leaking down the basement walls as Larry works. It's a morbid picture. I must have been nuts to take it. Some of the toys I finally bought for Dan were too hard for him to use. Bah Humbug."

The New Year's Day football games invaded every home while I drove the twenty minutes to visit Daniel on the unit. Dan was sick with a high fever and lay inside his room on his bed. He was obviously miserable, not being able to blow his nose because of residual paralysis in his mouth and nose. I rubbed his hot forehead and sang gently.

Just outside his door a staff was positioned to supposedly watch our son. The staff and a teenage patient played cards and howled with laughter. Rock music blared. Bright lights glared. I hated the insensitivity of the staff and detested a loud patient with her ridiculous gibberish.

"God," I prayed while driving home in the snow, "*I WILL NEVER* accept institutionalization. It makes no sense. *I WILL NEVER* accept that you are allowing people called 'staff' to care for my son when I want to care for him."

And He, who had left ivory palaces to enter this world of woe, seemed to ask in my heart, "Oh?"

The "*I WILL NEVER...*" Chapter 43

(Or, "*I WILL NEVER* engage in calisthenics again")

A financial fiasco lurked in fifteen-year-old David's world. He worked part-time on Friday night and Saturdays at a local restaurant and carefully saved his earnings. The financial "crisis" emerged when he took an entire Saturday off from work – with no pay – to be with his brother. It was a voluntary and caring expression of one brother for another.

Daniel was home twenty-five minutes before becoming violent and being returned to the facility.

I lay my head on the kitchen table, the winter sun casting shadows throughout the room. David, feeling humbled that his "best shot" had been rejected, retreated to work.

The next day David was peppered with hives.

Pride – the good kind – was dominant in each of us. David was proud that Dan idolized him. Larry and I were – on very few occasions – proud when we could handle Daniel. Becky was proud when she ducked extra quickly and missed a blow aimed by Dan in her direction.

175

It was pride, too, that would not let me rest until those working with our family knew about the Daniel we lost. I wanted the psychologist to literally know "where we were coming from." I wanted them to know the depth of our loss.

But above all, I wanted them to know we had produced a healthy, happy, beautiful, normal child. I wanted them to know he did not always have scars, broken teeth, an eye that veered, a crippled hand and leg, a drooling mouth, impaired speech, and aggressive behavior.

I wanted them to know we tucked in a well-mannered, gentle little fellow, and the same night we had a broken doll.

The new psychologist working with Daniel wanted to get a clue of Dan's pre-fall behavior and asked to view our recordings of earlier times. When he described himself as "anxious" to view the recordings, I knew we had a dedicated therapist. It was not until we were all seated in the family room and the first pictures appeared that I realized how foolish one feels rolling the mundane things of life before a psychologist who is taking notes.

The happy visual memories were devastating to view. I recorded in my diary, "After the therapist left, I felt like I'd been beat up."

In the seven weeks since hospitalization in the new hospital, Dan sustained: a broken hand, going to the emergency room twice in one day since he removed the bandage; a huge bruise on the groin area that I discovered while bathing him; tissue damage in his other hand from a fall on the ice; a mysteriously swollen foot that needed X-rays; a broken right index finger from having it slammed in the time-out door as he was being locked in; stitches in one hand; a chipped bone in his elbow which required a cast; two chipped front teeth, which went unreported; and a bad bruise on his left hand that was also closed in the time-out room door while his arm was still in the cast. There were numerous bouts of self-abuse. Restraints were used often.

The psychiatrist in charge of the children's unit summoned us for a meeting. He proposed an investigation by the Department of Children and Family Services to determine if abuse was involved. He explained, "If it's one of my staff, or if it's you, or if it's the checker at the local restaurant, I want to know." We concurred.

The investigator later reported that because so many people were involved in Dan's life and because of his self-abuse, as well as proneness to accidents, it was impossible to pinpoint any abuse.

A horrible month came to an appropriately horrid close as I sat alone in front of the television. I was filing my nails and only half listening to the preacher ranting on the screen in front of me. He concluded his sermon with, "It is never God's will that anyone be sick. You just need more faith to make them well."

I went upstairs to the bedroom to work on "faith-enlargement." As I lay back across the flowered bedspread, I tightly shut my eyes, contracted my shoulder muscles, and curled up my lip and nose as I tried to "believe more."

The phone brought me back to reality as an unknown lady sweetly introduced herself. She ever so kindly chatted, "I've heard of you. I have a daughter who is retarded, but she was actually healed at the cross. She'll be all right as soon as I can believe more." She exhorted me at length and offered to meet with me weekly to pray for my weak faith.

I thanked her for her interest and politely excused myself. I flopped back on the bed. In one hour I had been surrounded and shaken by a "believe harder" creed. The resulting guilt was overwhelming.

It was horrendous that Daniel was as he was, but the belief that he was in that condition because his mother did not have ample faith for him to be well was a more terrifying situation than I could bear.

I lay staring at the ceiling. A distant booming voice resounded in my ears as clearly as if I were hearing it for the first time as a Bible college freshman. "Oh, precious freshman," thundered Frank Sells, "don't have faith in your faith. Have faith in Jesus."

That was it. I had been so busy trying to conjure up a strong faith, I had forgotten the One in whom I was believing.

I did not squint my eyes tightly shut, neither did I contract neck muscles, nor did I scrunch my mouth as I prayed, "Oh, Father, *I WILL NEVER* fathom the simplicity of faith. It is just Jane, trusting Jesus. *I WILL NEVER* engage in spiritual calisthenics again."

And in my relaxed heart He seemed to say, "Oh?"

The "*I WILL NEVER...*" Chapter 44

(Or, "*I WILL NEVER* forget the candy box")

I had been "pulling rank" for four years. In my praying and pleading, I had often voiced, "Lord, I'm Daniel's mother. Surely You'll heal him because of his mother's prayers."

As I read about two sisters seeking the Lord Jesus to heal their brother in John 11, I noticed they used no arm-twisting. Instead, they said to Jesus, "He whom thou lovest is sick." My prayer for Dan changed after that. I began praying, "Lord, he whom Thou lovest is sick..." (sometime it feels good to pray in the King James Version).

Easter dawned with breezes of new hope. During Dan's afternoon visit he was visibly moved as his Daddy told the familiar story of Jesus' death and resurrection. He seemed to understand Gethsemane and suffering. When Larry read, "He is not here, He is risen!" (Matthew 28:6 KJV), Daniel shouted, "Yeah," and clapped for joy.

And then he grabbed a clock and hurled it at me.

The perplexing behavior never ceased.

As the first day of May approached, Dan asked to cancel his twelfth birthday. Later, we persuaded him to go through with it, and he requested a piñata. The therapist laughingly commented, "Beating a piñata is socially acceptable aggression."

While Dan whacked the hanging piñata with a stick, the rest of us cowered in safe corners.

Daniel soon began overnight visits home once a week. The first visit went well, with only a vase and a pot of coffee thrown at me. The next week, during his overnight visit, Dan awoke at 2:30 a.m. with diarrhea. While he struggled for an hour with Larry, the bathroom plus the inhabitants became putrefied after the physical and emotional diarrhea. I called the mental health facility, alerting them that Larry was returning Daniel. The staff questioned our judgment and stated, "We didn't think you were supposed to return him unless you had to."

Glancing at my dirty son and filthy husband still in "latrine-al" warfare, I replied, "They are on their way." The staff's reluctance had sounded strange coming from the same facility where Dan was allowed to go to school only 45 minutes a day, "because we feel more comfortable with that."

Although it was May, it was hard to convince one's soul that spring had indeed sprung. The blustery weather rattled the windows, and I sat on the sofa, knowing spring in Virginia was sunny and "daffodilish" – so different from this mess.

I fell to my knees by the big plaid sofa. Remembering the disappointment in Daniel's voice earlier that morning during a phone conversation, I railed to God, "If my earthly father were here, he would make Dan well and ease our breaking hearts. But you are here, and you are powerful, and you are doing nothing. NOTHING. *I WILL NEVER* believe you love me as much as you say you do because love is active. And you are doing NOTHING."

I lay my head on the cushion and breathed shallowly. My hand rested on my Bible that lay nearby when I heard the familiar clank of the mailbox.

Every morning – no matter what time I had my time of prayer and Bible reading – the mailman came. I had struggled with this rather mundane issue, feeling twinges of guilt when I put aside the Word of God to go fetch the mail. I thought the issue had been settled after the Lord seemed to ask me why I would lay aside His Word that is fresh every morning for stale mail.

But this morning was different. It was gruesome on the outside and on the inside, and the struggle was keen.

Clank. I did not lift my head from my arms, but I opened my eyes wide, and turning my head, I looked at the door. I needed to refine my excuse, so I sat straight up and prayed, "Today I'm getting the mail before I finish my prayer time. There just may be a prayer request from someone in the box today."

God did not believe that anymore than I did, but at the time it sounded feasible.

The cold, damp weather pelted my face as I leaned out of the door to retrieve the "prayer requests." After drying my face and hands, I examined the strange package that I had lifted from the box. No return address. No postmark. No zip code. Strange wrappings. Tons of tape.

I peeled off the wet, brown paper and gazed at the pink candy box. I gently opened the box, and a lovely wooden plaque fell into my lap. I read it out loud:

Heaven's Special Child

A meeting was held quite far from earth
"It's time again for another birth,"
Said the angels of the Lord above,
"This special child will need much love.
His progress may seem very slow;
Accomplishments he may not show,
And he'll require much extra care
From all the folks he meets down there.
He may not laugh or run or play;
His thoughts may seem quite far away.
In many ways, he won't adapt,
And he'll be known as handicapped.
So let's be careful where he's sent.
We want his life to be content.
Please, Lord, find the parents who
Will do this special job for You.
They will not realize right away
The leading role they're asked to play.
But with the child from above,
Comes stronger faith and richer love.
And soon they'll know the privilege given
In caring for this gift from Heaven –
Their precious child so meek and mild
Is Heaven's very special child."

My icy, defiant heart began to thaw around the edges. Curious as to who sent it, I carefully opened the box.

The little white folded piece of paper still rested on the candy box. As I unfolded it, my eyes beheld the handwritten signature –

All my love, Jesus.

Finally, I fell again before Him – this time with my face flat on the floor in utter reverence.

"Father," I whispered, "I am so sorry I accused you of not having an active love for me. Thank you for the love note. I love you, too."

I rose and carefully placed my sacred mail on an end table. I glanced at it often during the day and repeated again and again, "*I WILL NEVER* forget the lesson learned this morning. *NEVER*."

And He, who knows about fickle hearts, seemed to say, "Oh?"

The "*I WILL NEVER...*" Chapter 45

(Or, "*I WILL NEVER* forget wounded hands")

Sitting in the car, I cautiously instructed my second-born son, "When we go into the store for ice cream, should you blow kisses to strangers? Should you kiss the hand of the check-out girl?" Obediently, Dan answered, "No, Ma'am." With that established, Dan and I joyfully entered the large grocery store to buy ice cream for his parent's sixteenth wedding anniversary.

We hustled briskly to the frozen foods. I held the ice cream in one hand and Dan's hand with my other hand. I also prayed for a short checkout line.

Daniel tried to grab a fire extinguisher off of a pole as we headed toward the cashier, but he let go without causing a scene. I prayed even more for a short checkout line, knowing we were on borrowed time. When I handed the money to the cashier, Daniel slithered unnoticed to an empty checkout station close by. Over the P.A. system a familiar voice echoed throughout the store – "Hi, Mom, I love you." Clerks, with ears finely attuned to the amplification, whirled in their checkout stands. The manager quickly glared out of his elevated glass cage. Customers rallied up the aisles for a look.

Turning on my heels, I mustered an embarrassed grin. "Well, Daniel," I calmly said as if this were an everyday happening, "Thank you, and I love you, too."

Rushing out, I was proud of the way I had hidden my flustered feelings when a clerk yelled after us, "Ma'am, you forgot your ice cream."

Several weeks later we eagerly brought Daniel home for his home visit, although we had been warned of a new self-abuse behavior of his scratching the roof of his mouth until it bled. He was militant from the moment he entered our front door.

Late in the afternoon Larry, bone-weary from hours of struggling, carried Daniel to his room for another hour of locked "time-out." Daniel bit Larry's hands, clawed his face and eventually wrapped his legs around his daddy's, tripping him. As Larry lay on the floor, Daniel relentlessly attacked, and my husband calmly stated, "Jane Lee, you'll have to take over. My hand just broke."

Becky accompanied her daddy as he drove himself to the hospital. In fear and trembling I drove Dan back to the facility. I remembered, "Music soothes the savage beast," and so I bellowed every song I could think of. Daniel chimed in with "You are my sunshine, my only sunshine. You make me happy, when skies are gray..." I shook my head in disbelief, thinking how inappropriate the words sounded at the moment.

When I left the facility, four adults were restraining Daniel on the floor. I was anxious not only to leave that scene but also to get home and check on Larry.

Larry lay in the bright yellow bedroom, resting his casted hand on a pillow while Becky merrily chatted about the workings of a hospital. I closed the bedroom door and tried to listen to Becky's ceaseless chatter, my preoccupied mind with her daddy in the other room. "Hands can be fixed; broken hearts don't mend as quickly," I thought.

Becky scampered out to play, and I mechanically dusted the piano. "Thank You, God, that You can comfort Larry because You know how it feels to be a hurt Father. *I WILL NEVER* cease to marvel at Your comfort. NEVER."

And He, who understands wounded hearts and wounded hands, seemed to say, "Oh?"

The "*I WILL NEVER...*" Chapter 46

(Or, "*I WILL NEVER* be a loving wife")

Larry and I sat at the large table surrounded by discouraged mental health workers. I nervously doodled with a pen, and Larry stared at the doctor as he solemnly explained a new proposed treatment plan. The plan would confine Daniel to an area of isolation, hopefully making it impossible to aggress.

Larry and I viewed the small windowless cubicle tucked behind the kitchen at the end of the hall. In this tiny cinderblock room a mattress rested on the floor. A large clock and fire alarm hung in the larger area for staff. A long, heavy table separated Dan's half of the area from the staff's portion. An alarm bell was later installed so staff could summon help.

Daniel never left this "den." He used a bedpan in this room. He bathed in this room. He did schoolwork in this room. And he slept in this room.

I detested it.

Dan's only respite from this environment was his overnight visit home once a week. As Larry and I drove to the facility to pick up our son for his overnight stay, Larry sadly said, "You know, it is horrible having someone in the house who is constantly stalking you and conniving to hurt you, and you never know when he's going to attack."

When we arrived, the scene on the unit sickened us. An obese staff lay on the floor with his legs wrapped around Daniel to immobilize him. The cubicle was demolished, with the large table overturned. Food, a milk carton still oozing milk, and two overturned chairs were heaped on the floor. The staff member was bleeding from imprints that matched Dan's teeth.

We wrapped Daniel tightly in a blanket and transported him home. Larry and I were on guard duty most of the night, seeking to protect our other sleeping children.

Weary, we returned Daniel the next morning. As we entered the large hall, a staff member firmly announced, "Welcome back, Dan. You must go straight to your area and clean the mess you left last night." Daniel bolted from our three hands (Larry's hand was still in a cast) and wildly dashed toward the exit.

At such times I usually froze in my tracks. This time, however, I waxed bold and rushed toward my son, subduing him until staff and Larry quickly took over.

On the way home I felt victorious. I had actually asserted myself into the fray rather than freezing from fright.

While I silently basked in my victory, Larry unexpectedly queried, "Jane, why did you let go of him so soon?"

In slow motion I turned my head toward him in disbelief. The longer I dwelt on Larry's question, the more angry and hurt I became. I thought I had done valiantly. Larry went on to say that, although I had behaved bravely, he thought my timing was off a bit.

I carried my disappointment all week and spoke to my husband only when necessary.

I drove to a nearby shopping center and sat in the car and reflected over our sharp words. I recalled accusations hurled at one another in anger. The years of physical and verbal abuse from our son were taking their toll on us.

I fidgeted with the car blinker, and prayed, "Father, *I WILL NEVER* be able to be a loving wife when my heart is always throbbing with pain."

And He, who knows all about marriages and strained emotions, seemed to say, "Oh?"

The "*I WILL NEVER...*" Chapter 47

(Or, "*I WILL NEVER* let God remove another son")

Flipping through the out-of-date magazines in the doctor's crowded office, I grinned. "Boy, when a pap smear is the highlight of your week, your life must be the pits," I said to no one.

After the physical examination, the physician inquired if there was any stress in my life.

Cursively, I told about Daniel and our many moves. When I explained that Dan could not live at home, the caring doctor leaned forward and asked in amazement, *"You mean love was not enough?"*

Stunned, I did not know how to respond. Was that a subtle implication that if we had loved Daniel just a little more, he could be well? Sensing my dismay, the physician left.

Slowly dressing in the sterile room, I pondered, "Why wasn't love enough?"

Introspection ate away at my strength as I tried to measure my love. How could I love my children more than I did? I would lay down my life for each of them.

During my love-struggle, I comforted myself: David was blossoming into a sensitive man of God; Becky was "remarkably stable," said a teacher. We had loved *them* "enough."

Once home, I sat in the kitchen, scraping bits of food off the table into my hands and said out loud to the Lord, "You know mothering is the most influential role I'll ever have. I don't want to botch it up. *I WILL NEVER* understand why you limited my input into Dan's life. But I really want to pour everything I've got into David and Becky's lives."

It was late afternoon when the phone rang. My father-in-law spoke from his home in North Carolina. "We were at the Ben Lippen Bible Conference in Asheville, North Carolina all week. We investigated the residential high school at Ben Lippen. Would you consider David's coming here for high school? Pray about it."

Click.

Fire flashed from my eyes. I hissed to Larry, "*I WILL NEVER* have to pray about that. There's no way God is going to remove another son from our home."

I busied myself furiously mopping the kitchen floor. God seemed to ask, "Jane, if this high school were in my plan for David, would you let him go?"

I wrung out the mop with angry adrenalin; "God, we do not need to discuss this. I know this is not your plan."

I considered the issue closed when I flopped into bed that night.

My eyelids refused to stay closed. I thought about my first son – God's bringing us both through his difficult birth; his having been in nine different schools in nine years; my

191

longing for him to be in the same high school for three years; my desiring him to be in a Christian school. But I still wrestled.

The next day I kept fighting nagging thoughts about this Christian high school in North Carolina – so far from Springfield, Illinois.

In fact, that was all I thought about.

I dished up the grilled cheese sandwich in front of David and fearfully asked, "So, how do *you* feel about going to school so far from home?"

Taking a bite of his sandwich, my son explained, "Well, Mom, I would really like their sports program. And I do want to go to a Christian school. And I know it's great academically. But I can't go."

I breathed a sigh of relief and sipped my hot tea, "Oh? Why can't you go?" I asked nonchalantly.

"Well, 'cause who'll take out the garbage? And who'll rub Dad's back? And besides, I don't know how to tie a necktie."

I dished up the pickles in utter amazement.

It was a long week of praying. I was more relaxed than anyone since I knew that God would not remove another son from our home. It would be the ultimate put-down for me. It would be as if God were writing a commentary on my inept parenting. Surely, God would not displace me – nor replace me – with more STAFF.

I put the morning newspapers in my lap when David entered the living room. He brimmed with honesty, "Mom, I'm really scared. But I believe God wants me at Ben Lippen." I stared at him as he paused. "And, Mom, I want to be the one to tell Daniel."

I heard him singing in the shower as I fiddled with a tasteless cup of cold coffee. In my soul I knew the decision was a right one. It was just a very difficult one.

I pushed the vacuum cleaner perfunctorily over the rug while I prayed, "Father, *I WILL NEVER* understand Your ways. *I WILL NEVER* be able to explain this to others. *I WILL NEVER* get over this inferior feeling because You keep removing my children."

And He, who knows all about mothers' hearts, seemed to lovingly say in mine, "Oh?"

The "*I WILL NEVER...*" Chapter 48

(Or, "*I WILL NEVER* be able to thank you")

Becky was dressed in new "third-grader" clothes, and her excitement bubbled as she caressed her shiny lunch box. Daniel, home overnight, pounded on the front window mournfully screaming, "I want to go to a real school too. Why me? Why did I have to fall? Becky, please don't go to school..."

He successfully dampened the ardor of Becky's first day of school. It was not fair to Becky, but it was reality.

The weekend was gloriously warm, with the sunshine making shadows on the kitchen wall. Daniel was visiting Becky and me on a Saturday while Larry was en route to North Carolina with David to enroll him at Ben Lippen High School. After Dan's ceaseless attacks on Becky and after his pouring a pan of hot peas on me, I called a friend from our church for help.

Humiliated, I wrestled with Daniel in the back seat while Artie drove the car. I felt embarrassed because I needed help.

I had a first-born — at the age of 13 — on the road to a school very far away. I had a second-born son who had scalded my head that morning. Giving motherhood my best shot, I took Becky that afternoon to the circus. Note to self: do not sit next to the band, much less the drums, while nursing an off-the-chart migraine.

Larry was home the next weekend when Dan visited, and I felt more at ease. I took our son into the bright September air and pitched a wiffle ball at his oversized plastic bat. He laughed, and I enjoyed his presence. Suddenly, he missed the ball and rushed toward me with the bat. I did not run because I feared Daniel would run blindly into the street. I trotted backwards, trying in vain to capture the viciously swinging bat. Because I had one arm trying to protect my face and the other arm pursuing the enormous bat, I did neither well.

Becky, our shortstop, rocketed into the house, hysterically summoning her dad. Larry and I carried Dan's flailing arms and legs to his room for a time-out.

Becky stood behind me and patted my back while I sat shaking in the kitchen. I was not sure which hurt more – the beating or the burden. Both made for drooping shoulders.

Larry decided that we needed to return Dan immediately to the facility. We were in the bedroom getting a blanket to wrap around him to restrain him, when I heard him sweetly calling Becky's name from the kitchen. He almost sang her name. I "happened" in the room first and found Dan crouched with a butcher knife in his hand. I knew to reach slowly. Steadily, I reached for the knife, and he did not resist.

Becky's eight-year-old eyes were wide as she thought of what could have happened. Larry, visibly shaken, said, "That's it. Let's go."

The ride back to the mental health facility was strangely silent. In shock, we each sat staring out of the car windows. I held the fellow next to me in his blanket cocoon and silently prayed, "Father, *I WILL NEVER* be able to thank you enough for your protection of Becky today."

And He, who "inhabits the praise of His people" seemed to say, "You are welcome, daughter."

The "*I WILL NEVER...*" Chapter 49

(Or, "*I WILL NEVER* complain again")

Waving our white flags of surrender, we lay back, beaten in battle. The battle had been a long one, fought through clenched teeth and through floods of tears. It was as though we had been in an excruciating four year tug-of-war and in the end, were lying back in the mud with blistered hands, breathlessly lamenting, "We just can't pull any more..."

At the mental health facility Larry and I shifted nervously in our chairs around the large table. Being conquered by one's own son is not easy to admit.

The professionals concurred that because of the danger involved in the last several visits home, we should visit Daniel only on the unit.

I wanted to cry – from relief and pity – relief, because the battles at home would cease – pity, for a little boy whose only respite from a "cell" was his visits home several hours a week. I murmured to myself how much easier this would be if I did not love our son. Love tugs.

197

Dan's aggressions escalated, even in his controlled setting. He overturned the heavy table, quickly scaled it, and tore the fire alarm and large clock down with his one hand. Fewer and fewer staff were willing to be on duty their hour in Dan's area.

Not long after visits home were discontinued, we attended an Individualized Educational Program for our son. The smoke-filled room, permeated with the smell of coffee in Styrofoam cups, overflowed with professionals. An advocate, supposedly on our side, suggested there could have been a learning disability before Dan fell because there are a lot of left-handed people in our family.

She was on *our* side?

I stared this woman down at the insinuation that there had been a problem before his fall.

I lay awake at night dreaming of ways to make the morbid cell homey. The pictures I put on the cinderblock wall brightened it not a bit. A friend had painted a large picture of Snoopy and Peanuts characters on the wall, but Daniel quickly demolished it.

Because the Illinois winter was whistling under the door close to Dan's area, he was moved back to his previous room with the large window. The rules remained the same – he was never to leave the room and no one was to enter unless he went several days without aggression; he was under constant one-on-one supervision twenty-four hours a day; he ate; he bathed himself with a small pan of water; and he used a bed pan in the confines of this small room.

Dan sat on his bed next to the window while his teacher sat in the hall instructing him, using a blackboard installed on his door. A mattress was his only furniture (no box springs because he could use those as a weapon) and a chair from time to time, depending on his behavior. He was allowed no pencils, no toys, no clothes in his room, and no hardcover books. Tape on the floor marked the narrow boundary of the space where he could move – if he stepped over the tape, the door was locked because of threatening behavior.

When his food was brought on a tray, Daniel had to be seated on his mattress. When the door was unlocked, the tray was slipped just inside the door. Daniel was allowed to retrieve the food after the door was again locked. A rope hung from the doorknob so staff would not have to touch the knob.

This whole procedure – while necessary to prevent aggression – reminded me of feeding time at the zoo. I detested it.

While this treatment plan of virtual isolation was restrictive, it was a viable alternative to a "chemical straight jacket." The doctor could have sedated Dan and rendered him non-aggressive – but a vegetable. The weary staff took the more difficult route for them, hoping to see improvement in this boy who was brimming with productive potential but destructive power.

One bold cleaning lady who entered Daniel's room daily loved the Lord, and Daniel eagerly awaited her "mopping fellowship." They had the very same conversation each day as she mopped and Daniel stayed seated in his appointed corner. "Who's your best friend, Danny?" she asked. And he replied, "Jesus is. Who's your best friend?" And she smiled and answered, "Why, Jesus is." Daniel giggled and continued, "Ya know, I think He's supercalifragilisticexpialidocious."

Daniel never aggressed toward this lady until one day, after having been cautioned by a superior to refrain from this type of talk, she entered the room to mop. She was strangely silent. Daniel hurled a chair at her.

Arriving home, I tarried in the car for a moment. I thought about the tired staff that had sustained many injuries from my son.

"God, thank you for the people who work with such an explosive fellow. I know the work is hard and unrewarding. *I WILL NEVER* complain about staff again."

And He, who knows sanguine emotions, seemed to say in my heart, "Oh?"

The "*I WILL NEVER...*" Chapter 50

(Or, "*I WILL NEVER* live this one down")

"Calamity Jane" went shopping.

The therapist had mentioned that Daniel was leaving a mess on his mattress where he rested his plate to eat, and that he needed something more firm to eat on. The therapist suggested a hassock would offer more stability for his plate and could be used to write on during school hours, but would be soft enough that Daniel could not injure anyone with it.

It was a bitingly cold January day. Snow did not deter my shopping for a hassock. Something, however, got lost in the translation.

I merrily trekked to several stores and inquired about *hammocks*. Each salesperson responded the same way – glancing out of the window at the snow and asking, "A *hammock*?" After so many stores and questioning looks, I became agitated. At the last store, the salesman explained, "Lady, we don't have hammocks now. That's a seasonal item."

"Why on earth is a footstool a seasonal item?" I wondered, as I retreated to the domestic department.

Determined, I looked for something soft and sturdy as a substitute for the hassock. My eyes caught the clothesbaskets. They were lightweight, yet upside down they could serve as a table. I decide to test one. I had to be sure Daniel could not hurt anyone with it, so I hit it with my fist and bounced it off my head. I turned it upside down and knelt beside it, pretending to eat off of it. I was lost in my plastic world when gradually I peeked up to see the "hammock" salesman staring at me.

I stacked the yellow basket back into the other colored ones and left the store.

Dejectedly, I reported to the psychologist that I had been unable to get the desired hammock. He laughingly corrected my terms. "Mrs. Bateman, ask them for a *hassock.* I bet you'll have better luck."

I burst into laughter.

"Thank You for loving silly people. *I WILL NEVER* forget the joy and dismay over shopping for a hassock...or was it a hammock?"

And He, who said the earth is His footstool, seemed to laughingly ask, "Oh?"

The "*I WILL NEVER...*" Chapter 51

(Or, "*I WILL NEVER* understand fairness")

We stood on tiptoe as the plane landed and Becky wormed her way through the crowd to get a first glimpse of her older brother, David, returning from school in North Carolina for Christmas.

I spotted the tall boy doing a "jig" as his feet hit Illinois soil when Larry proudly nudged me, "There's our boy." This mature boy belonged to us, and as he wrapped his arms around his dad's neck, he began sobbing. Eventually, our tearful family got the security guard crying.

On Christmas Eve we took shopping bags of carefully chosen toys to Daniel. Christmas is bleak in a mental institution, and Daniel was the only patient there, except for one girl who refused to get out of bed.

The plastic, swirling racing track was clearly the hit of the evening, and even staff ventured into Dan's room to play. The tall staff turned to me and said, "Daniel knows that if it were not Christmas Eve, I would not be in this room."

When it was time for us to leave, Daniel did not scream.

Daniel and David embrace

This made it a very special Christmas, indeed.

By Christmas Day Dan had demolished most of his gifts, and the racing track was in pieces in the hall. He urinated on the rug, wrote obscenities on his wall, and threw milk. He shrieked as we left, devastated.

None of us spoke as we drove home. The heaviness in our car did not match the brightness of the night as the moon beamed on the snow-covered fields.

Emotions were pushed way down, hopefully to "stay put." We should have known better - they never "stay put." The sad, frustrated emotions simmered until New Year's Eve.

We had invited a lonely old man out to eat and had unwisely scheduled it after a visit to the mental health facility. The visit was horrendous. Dan went after David, and we unwisely corrected David for trying to defend himself. He ran out of the gym yelling, "Daniel can tear me apart, but you won't let me lay a finger on him!" Slamming the gym door, he retreated to the cold car.

"Was David right?" I wondered as I threw the basketball to Daniel. I wondered if we were subconsciously protecting Daniel from others, more than we were protecting others from Dan. Were we expecting too much from our other two children, who had neither the maturity nor commitment to Daniel that parents have?

Larry, Becky, and I joined David as he sat in the car to pick up our old gentleman friend. No one wanted to eat, much less together. We play-acted a tremendously hypocritical drama of joy. The old man was deaf, and it felt good to shout to someone.

When we arrived home, everyone sought sanctuary in his own room - except me. I stayed in the kitchen to think. I put my cold feet on the heat register and swiveled in the chair.

"Father, why didn't you just keep Daniel safely in the top bunk bed? Do you care at all? *I WILL NEVER* understand why you continue to allow this family to live in such turmoil."

And He, who cared deeply, seemed to say in my heart, "Oh?"

The "*I WILL NEVER...*" Chapter 52

(Or, "*I WILL NEVER* shake my fist again")

Some friends had given us money as a Christmas gift with the stipulation that it be used for a weekend together at a Christian Marriage Encounter conference. Larry busied himself in the basement, making Becky a pair of stilts, while I packed our suitcase.

This specially designed weekend, teaching communication techniques in marriage, was a glorious one when Larry and I were free to share long pent-up emotions with each other.

One written communication with Larry concerning the feelings I had the most difficulty sharing went something like this:

> *The feelings I have the hardest time sharing*
> *are my feelings of deep failure and*
> *inadequacy as a mother because of my*
> *inability to cope with Daniel at home. I feel*

weak when you seem to feel so confident in that situation. I feel like a thin layer of ice that one never knows whether or not it will break. I even feel cold like that, too. The feeling tastes like very weak coffee. I feel this every day, but it is exaggerated when Dan comes home to visit. I felt God was confirming my in-aptitude as a mother when He removed David from our home as well.

The feelings of inadequacy are nauseating. They are the color of liver bile. They are sluggish feelings - like phlegm.

I love the way you can make me feel strong. I love the way you accept my hurting and still love me. I love the way you believe I'm wonderful when I don't. Surely since I have to suffer, you are the best one in the world to suffer with. Your steadfast quality makes it bearable. I love you.

Another communication went like this:

I want to go on living with you although there have been many times I felt I could make it better on my own. I want to go on living with you because you are the gentlest man I've ever known. You are gentle to me like cotton is gentle to my skin. You love me even when I'm extremely unlovable, and you reflect God's love better than any visual aid. Your strength makes me feel like I'm on a cable chair being lifted up to the top of Maggie's Valley. Your strength makes me feel like a warm whirlpool is surrounding me. It tastes like a cup of hot coffee in the morning. You make me believe in myself. You make me feel capable and wonderful. That feeling is a brilliant green and yet tastes like lobster dipped into hot butter...

It was not only glorious to be together for a weekend but also to reach way down in our wounded souls and share.

"Father," I prayed, "*I WILL NEVER* descend from this mountaintop."

Crashing down from the mountaintop came only days later. Larry and I took Daniel out to get a haircut and a new pair of shoes. Nothing was simple with Daniel. Nothing. At the barbershop he called the stranger in the next chair "gay." Larry and I slid behind our newspapers, hoping no one could understand our son's slurring speech. Hairy snickers indicated Dan spoke all too plainly.

At the shoe store Dan bolted from our tight grasp and approached a couple with a brand new baby in an infant carrier. The proud, unsuspecting couple stopped to allow our "poor, handicapped child" to view their baby. Larry and I froze.

As the couple left, Dan went berserk, and we dragged him across the mall sidewalk and squeezed the kicking legs, swinging arms, pinching hands, and biting teeth into the car. Larry whisked us away, and three staff helped us get Dan - and his flailing extremities - into the unit.

When we arrived home later than expected, we found Becky had taken refuge at a neighbor's house. We did not know them well, but they had taken her in when she appeared at their door meekly saying, "I don't know where my Mom and Dad are...and it's dark." They fed her orange juice and a cinnamon bun. The cinnamon on her rosy cheeks made her look like a sugar cookie. I held her tightly and explained the long struggle with Daniel.

She understood. In one sad sense, it was our way of life to her.

I sat with her while she ate her Happy Meal that we had brought home. She hummed between bites and swung her legs in rhythm.

"Lord, why can't I be resilient like Becky? Why don't I ever feel like humming any more?"

I took a sip of Becky's milkshake and continued to pray, "Father, do I ever make You struggle with me? Do I ever shake my willful fist in Your face?"

Knowing the answers, I affirmed, "Father, *I WILL NEVER* fight against you again."

And He, who knows about willful hearts, seemed to say in mine, "Oh?"

The "*I WILL NEVER...*" Chapter 53

(Or, "*I WILL NEVER* cease to marvel...")

It was Valentine's Day.

Becky had made her daddy a crooked heart-shaped cake that made him sick, but she had delighted in the making of it. We never told her about the effects on her Daddy's stomach.

I cherished Daniel's crude homemade valentine. Tears dripped on this special card when Dan inquired, "Momma, do you really like it?"

"Ah, Dan, this is one of the most special Valentines I've ever received," I said, while patting his shoulder. We sang together the little chorus, "Jesus is my true valentine/His heart was pierced for me/I cannot tell why He loved me so well/but He proved it on Cavalry."

Daniel's tight fist socked me hard in the mouth.

On Saturday Larry visited Daniel alone. I had experienced a weepy day and felt a visit to the hospital would be more than I could handle.

211

I wallowed in my feelings of inadequacy all afternoon.

I finally put aside spools of thread from mending, and listened to my Valentine's Day gift to Larry. The words of the song spun themselves around my heart:

> *I am loved, I am loved,*
> *I can risk loving you.*
> *For the One Who knows me best*
> *loves me most.*

"Father, I am free to unconditionally love a boy who is often unlovely because you unconditionally love me. *I WILL NEVER* take this for granted."

And He, "whose heart was pierced for me" seemed to say in mine, "Oh?"

The "*I WILL NEVER...*" Chapter 54

(Or, "*I WILL NEVER* believe God knows what this is like")

"Unclean, unclean." I was tempted to yell as people scattered when Larry and I took Daniel out of his room at the hospital. Although we both had a firm hand on him as we walked down the hall, the staff still warned the other patients, "Danny is out. Get in your room."

We retreated back to Dan's room so other patients could roam freely and we aimlessly twirled paper cups on the floor for amusement.

It was not long until we were informed that the staff had voted unanimously that we were not to take our son out of his room when we visited.

The staff also threatened union action to protect them from giving Dan a bath one night a week.

Later, I sat in the mall, watching the people go by. I thought how we *all* felt in bondage to the treatment plan.

"Father, do You know what it's like to love somebody so much and want to do something nice for him, and then not be able to? Do you know what it's like to see Dan held captive by his raw emotions and now captive in his room? *I WILL NEVER* understand why you don't intervene."

And He, who wants to lavish "every good and perfect gift" on His unwilling children, seemed to say in my heart, "Oh?"

The "*I WILL NEVER...*" Chapter 55

(Or, "*I WILL NEVER* enjoy a home visit")

I felt comfortable with the two male staff and Daniel. All were in the back seat of our car. One staff was about six foot seven, and I could hardly see around his head as I backed out of the driveway to go to a nearby hospital for Dan's physical therapy evaluation.

The evaluation went well - almost. Then Daniel initiated the battle, and the alert staff hurled him to the floor. Everyone bled. Nurses, pretending to be busy, stared. Waiting patients peered from behind sheeted curtains.

The conflict was a long one. It was a half-hour of restraining and resisting, bleeding and screaming, kicking and biting. Tired staff took turns confining Daniel to the floor.

I sat on the floor, trying to do my part in restraining, wondering how we were going to get this hysterically out-of-control person back down those long hospital corridors, down an elevator, and across two parking lots to the car.

I whispered to the tall staff as he struggled with Dan on the floor, "He loves a wheelchair. Let's borrow one, and you wheel him down while I get the car."

I gathered up coats, shoes, and socks and ran to get the car, being spurred on by adrenaline pumping furiously through my body.

Pulling up to the front door of the hospital, I noticed the tall staff pushing the wheelchair. One staff sat in the wheelchair holding Dan, who was bound Lazarus-style in a hospital sheet. I was ecstatic that I had missed the ride with them on the crowded elevator.

The warfare continued all the way back to the facility where Dan was toted mummy - fashion to his room.

Although it was early in the day, I felt weary. Physically and emotionally depleted, I called Larry at a nearby church and explained I could not minister with him that afternoon because I could not stop crying.

He understood.

I reclined on our bed and noticed the empty suitcases leaning against the wall. My long-anticipated trip home to Virginia to see my parents dimmed in my soul.

Realizing that my leaving the next day after such a difficult morning with Daniel might be unsettling for him, Larry and I returned in the afternoon to the unit to tell Dan of my impending trip home.

I peered through the small window in his locked door. Dan waved and sobbed, "You're going to Virginia without me? Please don't go without me. Please take me. Oh, Momma, please..."

I squeezed Larry's hand and said, "I can't handle this."

When I fled down the hall to the car, staff stopped me. The tall man, who had known the torture of the morning, comforted me. I remember being amazed at how far up his shoulder was to cry on.

I crawled into the car and rested my head on the steering wheel.

"God, why should I try anymore? Why keep visiting out here? Why force myself to come three times a week to this morbid place only to leave emotionally emaciated? Why don't I just abdicate? *I WILL NEVER* enjoy going on my own home visit now. I feel too guilty about leaving Dan."

And He, who knows all about the salve of home and parents, seemed to say, "Oh?"

The "*I WILL NEVER...*" Chapter 56

(Or, "*I WILL NEVER* balk again")

Daniel disappeared on his bicycle and headed toward the interstate. Security cars, four staff, as well as Larry, pursued in different cars. I nervously stayed by the busy interstate with other staff, watching the speeding traffic.

Larry found his son who eventually had wrecked on his bicycle. Larry scolded, "Son, that was a dangerous thing to do. Where were you going?"

"Daddy, I was only riding to Virginia. That's all. Remember my girlfriend from second grade? Does she still live in Virginia? I bet she wouldn't like me now..."

It was only a few days until Daniel destroyed his wall with a new "indestructible" leg brace. After the pieces of the demolished brace were removed from his room, he thrust his bare foot through the plaster, bending the steel mesh behind the three-foot hole.

Morale of those working with our son wrecked, capsized, and submerged. Daniel's mother was not unscathed by the emotional decline.

But the NEATEST THING HAPPENED.

It had been a sad session with the therapist - the kind of session when I wondered who should remain at the mental health facility, Daniel or me. I drove aimlessly around our city while a spiritual tug-of-war raged in the car.

The Enemy seized the moment and began his picking. Actually, pecking seems more descriptive. The foe seemed to cynically interrogate, "Look at you. Victorious, aren't you? You mean you are still planning to speak at Christian Women's Club tomorrow? What are you going to tell them - how victorious you are in the battle? And how good God is? What's He done for you today?"

The Lord Jesus seemed to whisper in my heart, "My little lady, you need to go home."

I burst into the kitchen, slung my purse on the doorknob, and blubbered, "Larry, I can't speak tomorrow. I have no victory. You'll have to speak for me."

Taking my hand, my husband tenderly reminded me, "Honey, victory is obedience. Victory is not always a gushy feeling."

I knew the theology was correct, but the application did not appeal to me. So I continued, "But Larry, I'm sick of hurting. I want joy. A light heart. I'm tired of this heaviness."

And he, who had suffered much, held me close and gently whispered, "Dearest Jane Lee, I am learning that you can have a pain in your heart and a settled peace in your soul at the same time because the Shepherd is in control."

When I speak throughout the country and tell our story, more women comment on that statement than any other:

*You can have a pain in your heart and
a settled peace in your soul at the same
time because the Shepherd is in control.*

I snuggled close and tarried in Larry's arms a long time. "Peace and pain...I do have both. I really do have both," I mused.

As I sat on the platform the next day waiting to speak, I prayed, "I want to thank You for the settled peace in my soul even though I have continuous pain in my heart. *I WILL NEVER* be reluctant to minister again because I feel sad."

And He, who spoke about peace during a painful earthly ministry, seemed to say in my heart, "Oh?"

The "*I WILL NEVER...*" Chapter 57

(Or, "*I WILL NEVER* pray again")

Larry set the tables up for our garage sale while I sorted through clothes. I held up the blue suit which topped David's ankles now and turned to put it in the mounting "for sale" pile. But a twinge of guilt grasped my heart first. Would selling this Sunday suit, instead of saving it for Daniel, blatantly be saying to the Lord that I did not think Dan would ever be well enough to wear it? It seemed so final.

I battled for a while in the bedroom. I tried to distinguish between faith and facing reality. I lay the blue suit aside and slowly folded the colorful bedspread, sticking the price on it with masking tape. I could not understand why my gut felt like I was sorting through the belongings of someone who had died.

I listened to cheery music when Larry busily entered the bedroom with a piece of paper. "How's this sound, 'For Sale, Twin bed, Good condition.'" My bare feet squeaked as I quickly whirled on the hardwood floors to face my husband.

221

"Whose bed are you selling?" I asked.

"Dan's bed. He doesn't come home any more. I can visualize this room as a study for you to write the book you've been talking about," he nonchalantly explained.

My emotions hemorrhaged.

I jumped over the piles of clothes and ran into the kitchen yelling, "Larry. I'm wrestling over a Sunday suit, but you are selling his bed? Why don't you just bury him?"

I fled out of the back door and sat on the ground, leaning against a tree. I wiped my nose with a leaf.

Totally surprised by my reactions, Larry sat stunned at the kitchen table.

After my bleeding emotions were under control, I entered the back door. Three family members cringed, waiting for more maternal erupting. I tried to explain why I had overreacted, though I was not sure myself. Sensing how deeply I felt about the issue, Larry retracted the newspaper ad.

Later, I heard my husband explain to someone else that it was difficult for him to pass the empty room and empty bed, and he thought making it into a study would ease the pain. I had been so charged with emotion, it had never occurred to me to see the situation from Larry's point of view.

After peddling our wares on Saturday, the sweet balm of relief dripped on our hearts on Sunday.

The small, hard-of-hearing elderly man with the glistening white hair cornered me by the piano at church. He brimmed with excitement because he had asked to speak at prayer meeting on Wednesday night and "have a prayer meeting for Daniel similar to the upper room prayer meeting," he explained.

At the midweek prayer service he looked like a miniature prophet behind the pulpit. His shaking hands, trying to steady the small cards that contained his notes, betrayed his age.

After his lengthy sermon the group prayed for Daniel.

Our next visit with our son lasted only ten minutes due to his explosive behavior. The nurse confirmed that it had been a horrid week.

Larry and I drove home dejected.

Disappointed.

Devastated.

"Larry," I carefully said, "I don't want to give old Mr. Smith the bad news. He just knew God would do something."

My thoughts turned heavenward.

"Father, praying seems to be a mockery. We pray - things get worse. *I WILL NEVER* pray again."

And He, who delights in communicating with His children, seemed to ask in my heart, "Oh?"

The "*I WILL NEVER...*" Chapter 58

(Or, "*I WILL NEVER* forget the love in the sanctuary")

The small white-haired "prophet" met me again by the piano. He shifted from one foot to the other and rested his hand on the open top of the grand piano towering over us. Reflecting on the apparent unchanged behavior of my son, I feared Mr. Smith would feel disappointed in the results of his "upper room" prayer meeting. He spoke softly in an aged high-pitched voice, "Little girlie, I've been thinking more about your boy." I smiled down at this short man who called me "little girlie." His false teeth clicked a bit as he said, "Do you think they could possibly take some of my brain and transplant it into Daniel? You see, he's a youngin' and has a whole life ahead of him. I'm old. I've lived a full life. I'm kinda all used up. I'd even be willing to pay for part of the surgery. Think about it, little girlie."

I squeezed his arm but could not speak. I sank into the front pew and stared at the purse on my lap. "Father," I prayed silently, "he's never even met Dan and yet he's willing to lay down his life."

Father seemed pleased at such love spilling over in the sanctuary.

In not too many months, Mr. Smith joined the Lord Jesus in the Upper Room.

I sat in the small chapel and listened to the eulogy. Silently, I talked to Father, "*I WILL NEVER* forget the visual aid Mr. Smith gave to me about sacrificial love."

And He, who sacrificed everything to die in my place, seemed to ask, "Oh?"

The "*I WILL NEVER...*" Chapter 59

(Or, "*I WILL NEVER* play the martyr again")

"I have even suggested that the possibility of brain surgery performed on this already damaged brain might be an approach. Of course, I realize the risky nature of this, the guarded prognosis of this, the political difficulty of this, as well as the most basic question of where in the brain should one inflict further damage to balance the impulsively hostile child," wrote a consultant in Illinois to another doctor in Massachusetts.

Surgery was not considered feasible enough to pursue; the vast amount of drug studies revealed little, and the previous behavior modification program brought only short term and minimal results.

External restraints were applied because Dan's internal restraints were insufficient. A leather belt with tethers attached to oven mitts on his hands limited his ability to attack. He could only go across the grounds to school for a brief time and visit at home for several hours with staff along.

His mobility, however, was sometimes more swift than we anticipated. Once, Dan became angry, fled down the hall, and smashed an IBM typewriter - all with restraints and oven mitts on.

While Daniel wore his restraints at all times when he was out of his room, sometimes four-point restraints were needed. This type of restraint tied his hands and feet to the bed and was used only when self-abusive behavior was out of control.

"On guard" when oven mitt detached from belt

Knowing when he was in four-point restraints was one of the most difficult parts of the hospitalization for me. My heart felt as if it too was in four-point restraints.

It was on one such occasion that I called the mental health unit to check on Daniel. The curt staff stoically explained our son had been in four-point restraints all night, and if he continued picking at the stitches in his face, he would be tied down again. I crumbled by the phone. The morbid information had been given in rote fashion, and my heart was grieved beyond measure at the apparent coolness of the staff.

I held the phone in my hands. Sobbing uncontrollably, I screamed to God to soothe my broken heart. I read in Psalms about the loving kindness of God and promptly doubted His loving kindness was as long-suffering as His Word proclaimed. I recorded in my diary, "Grieving makes me tired."

By late afternoon I had decided not to tell my husband about the problem with Dan. Larry had been unusually busy in ministry, and I decided I could cope alone, at least this time.

I put on fresh makeup, hoping it would disguise any hurt reflecting in eyes. When Larry came home, he reacted edgy and irritable to mundane occurrences. He picked at me, and I picked at him. It was not warfare but a subtle simmering of combative souls. It was not long until the full explosion. After the tears and harsh words were flushed out, the real issue surfaced. I cried into Larry's shoulder, "I'm sorry, but I tried to be strong and keep all this to myself. But I just can't. Dan was tied down for twelve hours. He'll probably be tied down more because he's being uncooperative. The thought nauseates me. I didn't want you to have to know all this..."

My husband lovingly looked at me. He hesitated before he spoke, "Jane Lee, I knew about this yesterday. I saw him in those restraints, and I knew he'd be in them all night. I was trying to keep this from you because it burdens you so."

As Larry held me close, I silently prayed, "Father, we were both trying to carry a burden alone that we were meant to share. *I WILL NEVER* play the martyr again and try to carry something alone that I was supposed to share with my husband."

And He, who said His yoke was easy, seemed to say in my heart, "Oh?"

The "*I WILL NEVER...*" Chapter 60

(Or, "*I WILL NEVER* soar with eagles")

Terror struck our hearts when the unit psychiatrist called to inform us that Daniel had signed papers for his discharge. Dan rescinded the "request" before his dad got to the unit but went on to sign the release papers several more times. He rescinded each time after persuasive talks by the staff, but each incident scared the daylights out of me.

I decided that if we ever had to prove in court why he needed to be hospitalized, I would suggest that Dan and the judge retire alone to the chambers and see who later emerged with the gavel – whereupon, I would rest my case.

I was reeling from the "release" papers when I ministered at a local church at a mother/daughter banquet. While I was gathering up my things to leave, a lady approached me. She took my hand and said, "You know, honey, I feel so sorry for you having a boy in a mental health facility. I used to work in something like that, and I said I'd rather my daughter grow up to be a prostitute than live on a mental health unit."

I am not sure how I responded verbally, but my eyes glazed over, and I quickly left. I crawled behind the steering wheel in the dark parking lot. The May breezes sifted through the open car window against my wet face.

Our friend Carl was dying of a brain tumor. And as he clung to life by a web, I felt jealous. "God, it's not fair that Carl will soon be freed from suffering and Dan will still be strapped in the crippled temple he calls home. Carl will be liberated from bondage - and Dan will remain a slave. It just isn't fair. Why didn't you call Dan home when you had such a good opportunity?"

I tacked on my pious smile and went to church. Our minister prayed "for our brother Carl who is dying." I leaned forward on the piano bench, uncomfortable in my spirit. I remembered having prayed for a gentle touch with hurting people, and yet I was seething with envy for a dying man. "Humph," I scowled with eyes closed, "why is he praying for 'our brother Carl' when he should be praying for Daniel who is rotting in a mental institution."

I was not proud of myself for spewing all of that.

Driving home, I said little to my family while they chatted about spring and flowers and birds.

"*I WILL NEVER* understand how God can let this go on year in and year out."

And He, who said we could "mount up with wings like eagles" seemed to say, "Oh?"

The "*I WILL NEVER...*" Chapter 61

(Or, "*I WILL NEVER* wallow in guilt again")

"Failure, Jane. You're a failure." That is what I saw written on the sign at the entrance to the mental health facility. There was no sign, of course, but it still seemed to mock me.

Every parent seems to struggle with guilt from time to time, but my seven year battle with the "if onlys" had been like a tsunami: *If only* my labor had not been induced, *if only* I had breast fed him, *if only* I had spent more time with him after his baby sister came, *if only* I had equipped him better in his early life to face trauma, *if only* I had disciplined him more, *if only* I had disciplined him less, *if only* we had not bought bunk beds...

In *The Hurting Parent*, Margie M. Lewis describes the guilt dilemma:

> *Of course it is a natural reaction for a hurting parent to re-examine himself or herself in search of some explanation. But too much and too close scrutiny,*

with the magnification of hindsight, can blow many
things out of proportion. We begin to dwell on what
went wrong and overlook what went right. The result
is an overload of unwarranted guilt.

This "unwarranted guilt" had bled into every facet of my life.

Because of my lingering guilt, I scrutinized my other children's behavior under a microscope lest there be any abnormal behavior.

I was curling my wet hair around ugly rollers while listening to the radio. The devil crept around unusually busily that morning and cynically whispered, "If God's grace is so sufficient, why isn't it sufficient enough so Dan can live at home? You really blew it, Jane." I replied out loud, "But I did the very best I could." Not to be outdone, the Enemy mocked, "Yes, you did. But your best just wasn't good enough, was it?"

The Enemy was very persuasive indeed.

My shoulders sagged beneath my blue robe. I fiddled with the rollers when the voice on the radio pierced my being. In essence the experienced doctor explained that God was the Perfect Parent. He had created His first child and put him in a perfect environment, and Adam *still* shook his fist in God's face. It was not God's fault.

As I heard that, the layers of heavy guilt peeled off, NEVER to come back again. The rollers fell to the floor as I knelt by the piano, "Oh, dear Perfect Parent, I am so sorry about how Your children turned out. But You are not to blame" (imagine me trying to comfort God). And it seemed as if He answered, "And dear parent of three, surely you made mistakes. But they were not fatal ones. I want to lift the guilt from off your heavy heart once and for all."

My tears of relief would not stop. I look back at that morning as a turning point in my life. When I speak around the country to hurting moms, they comment on how freeing that is to them as well: God was the Perfect Parent, and His children didn't turn out well either.

"Father, *I WILL NEVER* forget the release I experienced this morning. And *I WILL NEVER* listen to the Enemy's jabber again."

And He, the Perfect Parent whose heart was broken by His children, seemed to say, "Oh?"

The "*I WILL NEVER...*" Chapter 62

(Or, "*I WILL NEVER* finish writing this book")

"*I WILL NEVER* finish writing my book." I stated as I slid dirty dishes into the frothy water. My eyes glanced at a small paper above the sink, "Life Message: Sharing with others how God is using my weaknesses to conform me to His Son."

I argued, "But Father, how can I share with others what you are doing when I don't know what you are doing? You know it is illogical and does not make one bit of sense..."

Conform me to His Son? Would that hurt? I was content to be a rather generic Christian if being conformed was a painful process. I didn't mind suffering if it didn't hurt.

I slumped onto the sofa and held the newspaper in my lap. I pondered the positive lessons God had taught us in the past seven years: the new tenderness of heart He had worked in each of us; the glimpses of His Father-heart that we could not have seen except through suffering; the new sense of His suffering when separated from His Son; the shift in our priorities; the widening of our world; the new insights on emotions; the freedom to express our feelings; the new areas to trust Him; the soothing of His presence upon our pain; the vividness of His Word, especially in the Psalms; the deep fellowship of other Christians; our expanded ministry to others who hurt, and a renewed longing for Heaven.

I set aside the unread newspaper and reflected on all those blessings that had penetrated our lives over the years. We had hardly noticed.

There had been growth and untold blessings that only seemed to come through Father-filtered suffering.

You might want to read that last sentence again because it is one of the most important ones in the book. No one could have orchestrated "beauty from ashes" but God.

One night after supper, I viewed the dishes on the table and found it easier to sit. Becky, not wanting to practice piano, decided to chat with me at the table.

"Momma, what is the biggest thing you'd give to get Daniel well?"

I was stunned and sobered by the question. After a few brief moments I answered, "Oh, Becky, I'd gladly give myself." She responded, "No, that's not what I mean. Would you give up your piano or your book you are writing?"

How does one explain to a ten-year old that one would give up EVERYTHING?

I tried to adjust my thinking down to her level, and I said, "Becky, they could take my book and my piano...but mostly, I'd trade places with Daniel if that would make him well." Still not satisfied, she demanded, "What I mean is, what is one of your most valuable possessions?" And I quickly answered, "Why, you are." And her brown eyes widened as she queried, "You mean, you'd give ME for Daniel?"

I hugged her and assured, "Oh, Becky, I could never give you or David up for anything."

She ran off to play, and I could hardly comprehend such an awful thing as giving up one child for another. "*I WILL NEVER* understand how God gave up His Son in my place."

And God seemed to say in my heart, "I did it willingly, too, daughter."

NO MORE *I WILL NEVERS!* Chapter 63

The mental health system in Illinois had given it their best shot. And now it was time to move on. We all hoped fresh staff in a new state would give us a renewed impetus to keep going.

Daniel, accompanied by weary staff, flew in a chartered plane to Atlanta, Georgia. Daniel kissed the ground when he disembarked (and I'm sure the relieved staff wanted to as well).

Because his reputation preceded him, seven new staff members were assigned to him. Can you imagine seven staff assigned for just one boy?

It was difficult for the new facility to find a psychologist willing to work with Dan and our family, but a highly respected doctor from Florida flew once a month to counsel with Daniel and to try to keep our family and the new staff on an even keel.

After his first visit with Daniel, this doctor - for whom we will always be grateful - was flying back to Florida with a ripped shirt and broken glasses. A seatmate asked what he did for a living. He explained he was a psychologist. The fellow passenger obviously was intrigued with the doctor's appearance, which did not seem to match his profession.

As they discussed Daniel, the traveler - who worked in some aspect of security - suggested a stun gun to keep Dan under control. The positive side of that would be no one had to touch him and risk being injured, but it would still immobilize Dan momentarily.

Larry reacted with extreme caution at this new idea. He told the doctor and staff that they could not use the stun gun on his son unless they used it on Daniel's father first. The doctor said it was most effective when applied to the abdomen. Larry told the doctor to use it on him, and he would not push it away, but that he would be "coming after you like Daniel would with everything he's got." Larry and the doctor struggled but the doctor ended up on the floor with Larry on top of him and at his throat. Although disoriented, Larry would have been able to injure the doctor if he had so desired. Larry concluded that the stun gun may give time for the staff to react to Daniel's "stunningly" violent aggressive episodes without Daniel being harmed.

We reluctantly gave our permission and felt a small amount of relief when it was determined that only a few appointed staff were to use the stun gun. Stringent rules were in place to make sure the tool was not overused. It was not long until pictures of Daniel's burned abdomen revealed the stun gun was being used often and on other parts of his body.

The doctor and Larry (neither of whom had used the stun gun on Daniel) were separately "interviewed" by the Georgia Bureau of Investigation. The investigator requested the pictures in our possession of scars on Daniel's body for his report – and *promised* to return them. He did not. After that this measure of control was discontinued.

Daniel was no respecter of persons with his threats and aggression. The damage he inflicted on himself, staff, other patients, and family increased as he grew older and his size increased. Puberty had complicated matters even more.

The new treatment plan included restraining him in a large chair (picture a recliner on wheels) with both hands in oven mitts as well as leather wrist restraints that were secured with chains to a belt around his waist. His legs were also shackled to the chair.

The plan included lessening food intake in order to reduce his weight and strength. This was hard for me as a mother because one of his only pleasures was eating.

A staff member met me at a local McDonald's to discuss how things were going. He admonished, "Mrs. Bateman, I don't understand why you want to bring him treats. He doesn't deserve treats. Why do you want to bring clothes that match? He doesn't deserve that either. He's evil. It's so unfair and immoral that so much state money is going for one patient when there are others who want to be helped."

As we continued discussing Daniel's draining "the system" as well as staff, he seemed to imply no one would regret Daniel's demise. I couldn't tolerate one more minute with this man.

See Jane explode.

The staff member, as well as customers, saw a whole different side of this momma. To be honest, I saw a whole different side of myself.

I ranted and yelled, "Don't you ever call him evil. He had a head injury. You know that. I'm his mother. Mothers fix snacks for their children and buy them clothes. I hate what you're saying. HATE IT!"

He didn't back off – nor did I – and before we came to blows, I ran out one door and he walked out through another.

Daniel was scheduled to come home on Thursday nights for home visits. Although accompanied by four staff to protect us, it seldom went well. More often than not, he was taken out in a straightjacket type restraint, wailing and pleading not to go back to the hospital.

On one particular Thursday night, Daniel and I were sitting in the floor of our family room playing UNO. The four staff tried to give us some private family time while staying nearby in another room just in case I needed help.

Because Daniel could hold his cards in his left hand but could not pick out one with his paralyzed right hand, I improvised. I took a small loaf pan and filled it with dry rice. His cards stood up in the dry rice, freeing his left hand to retrieve a card.

Things were going well…until a staff member yelled from the kitchen, "Only 10 more minutes, Dan, 'til you go back to the hospital." I knew the minute he said it I was in major trouble. Before the staff had finished his sentence, Daniel threw the pan and rice in my face at a short distance – which is akin to being pummeled by iron pellets. Because I could not move for the pain in my eyes and face, he reached quickly for my turtleneck and twisted it around my neck and ground my head into the carpet. All with one hand. Staff and Larry jumped simultaneously to pry Dan's hand from around my neck. The more they pulled my boy's hand, the tighter

Daniel twisted the sweater around my neck and pushed my face into the carpet.

Eventually, they got him off of me and into the state van. I'm not sure who was howling louder – Daniel or me. Our family dreaded Thursday nights and it took days to recover emotionally and physically from the trauma before Thursday rolled around again.

It had been 17 years since Daniel fell. Seventeen years. I was too weary to even say, "*I WILL NEVER…*"

THE END OF THE BEGINNING... Chapter 64

I am convinced we would not be alive to write our story if we had not had help from the field of mental health. Although we disagreed with some treatment plans (and there were many), and while we found some staff hard to like, we are still extremely grateful that they were there for us – and for Daniel.

There are families all over our country dealing with an aggressive person in their home. I know because I hear from them. There are spouses who are dealing with stroke victims who are aggressive. There are parents who are dealing with an aggressive child.

Because the mental health system in our country is very different from our "Daniel years," less help is available now. There is little, if any, help for those families.

Unfortunately, the mental health system is broke.

After fighting our own battle for so long, we desperately tried to get on with our lives.

David graduated from Moody Bible Institute and married his beloved Laurie, a fellow student. Daniel was an honorary groomsman, though he could not attend the wedding.

Becky met her beloved Patrick at the youth group of First Baptist Atlanta. They too eventually married. Daniel could not attend that wedding either.

It is amazing to me that both Laurie and Patrick knew the unusual family they were marrying into and still chose to do it.

After seminary David and Laurie brought forth our first grandchild, Stephen. Because of so much heartache over the years, a new baby was welcomed with untold joy.

The little family had come from the midwest to Atlanta for Christmas. Daniel reveled in his new title of "uncle" and counted the minutes until he could see his nephew. The more excited Dan got, the more nervous the rest of us became. We knew there would have to be parameters about how close Uncle Dan could get to baby Stephen. We also knew the explosions that could occur because of those very precautions.

Daniel came home for a brief visit, and it was not long until he asked the dreaded question, "Can I hold the baby?"

I'm not sure if it were staff or the new parents or the new grandparents, but someone gingerly answered him, "Oh, Daniel, that is just not a good idea…"

Daniel went berserk. Staff tried to thread him into the restraining blanket as he kicked and screamed, "Please. I just want to hold him. I won't hurt him. I promise I won't hurt him."

He was carried out to the state van to be returned to the hospital.

It was a brutal scene. The protectiveness I felt toward this baby and the longing I had for Daniel to be near him crashed in my soul.

As per usual, each emotionally battered family member found refuge in a secluded place in the house where we tried to work through our turmoil and our tears with Dan's mournful screams of disappointment reverberating in our ears.

I was most concerned about our daughter-in-law, Laurie. Larry, David, Becky, and I had witnessed such explosions through the years, and were a bit more prepared to deal with such outbursts. But Laurie had not witnessed such furor. After getting my own heart quiet, I sought out baby Stephen and his mother.

I found Laurie sitting in a rocking chair cradling her baby. As tears streamed down her face, I knelt beside her and whispered, "I am so sorry you had to see that. I am just so very sorry."

The back and forth motion of the chair kept the baby quiet while Laurie spoke, "If holding my baby would have made him well, he could have held my baby."

I left the room, speechless.

****

Time moved on.

Today, David and Laurie, Becky and Patrick are in ministry and have a total of 8 children.

One of the greatest miracles of our lives has been the fact that the "Daniel years" were used in David and Becky's lives to make them the servants of God they are today.

And Daniel?

He once told me, "When I get to heaven, *I WILL NEVER* hurt anybody ever again."

At age 24, both became a reality.

Daniel lives happily ever after.

Physically and emotionally whole.

We would not have *chosen* the years of suffering.

We would not have *missed* them.

I WILL NEVER be able to thank God enough for all He taught our family through Daniel.

And that he called me Momma.

**"For *God Himself* has said,
'*I WILL NEVER*' leave thee
nor forsake thee."** Hebrews 13:5

NOTE TO MY GRANDCHILDREN

Stephen, Sarah, Shanleigh, Summer, and Ruth Bateman;
Morgan, Harrison Daniel and Kathryn Clough,

God has placed you in a unique family. Perhaps, our family
is more unique than most. (I guess most families think that
but we really are)

I know each of you has heard bits and pieces of our "family
story." This book details about our time with your Uncle
Daniel. Some of these details may be more than you can
handle until you are older.

I hope you will take with you a few things from this book for
your own life.

First, Jesus can get you through anything — even when your
feelings are slow to catch up to that fact.

Second, it is not a wise thing to say to God, "*I WILL
NEVER.*"

I hope one by-product of reading the complete story is that
you will understand why we have asked that you not sleep in
the top bunk at camp or sleepovers. There are thousands of
children taken to the emergency room each year after a fall
from a bunk bed and we want you safe. I hope you pass this
desire along to your children someday. But that is up to you.

Each of you has brought Pappy and me more joy than you
can imagine. To watch you grow spiritually by such huge
leaps and bounds makes our hearts sing! Just the thought of
each of you makes us smile.

You are my delight. *I WILL NEVER* get over the fact that I get to be your grandmother. You are greatly cherished.

Always in your corner,

Grandma Jane

Back Row: Larry, David and Laurie Bateman; Rebekah, Patrick and Harrison Clough.
Front Row: Jane, Stephen, Shanleigh and Summer Bateman; Kathryn Clough, Sarah and Ruth Bateman, and Morgan Clough.

*Dear Mom, You <u>do not</u> know how <u>heartbroken </u>I am about
hitting you in the mouth. I am really, and I mean really sorry.
I haven't been able to sleep well, all week. What happened
last week, was fifteen years of angry feelings all built up
inside. I've made a 'vow' with <u>myself </u>and with <u>the Lord Jesus</u>
that I will verbalize more things to you.*

Love,

Your second born son,

Daniel James Bateman

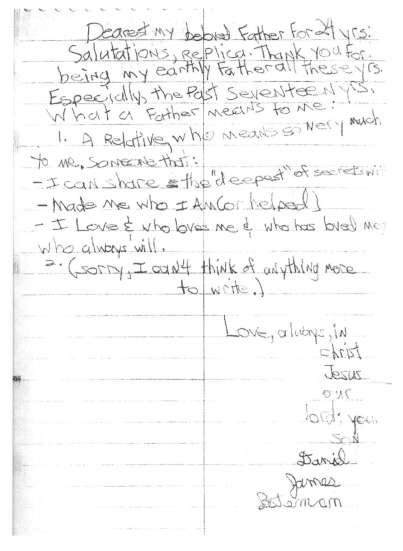

Dearest my beloved Father for 24 yrs: Salutations, Replica. Thank you for being my earthly Father all these yrs. Especially, the Past Seventeen yrs. What a Father means to me:

A Relative, who means so very much to me. Someone that:
- I can share the "deepest" of secrets with
- -Made me who I am (or helped)
- - I love & who loves me & who has loved me who always will.
2. (sorry, I can't think of anything more to write.)
- Love, always, in Christ Jesus our lord; your son
- Daniel James Bateman

BIBLIOGRAPHY

Lewis, Margie M., *The Hurting Parent*, (Grand Rapids, Michigan: Zondervan Publishing, 1980), page 95